COLLEGEVILLE BIBLE COMMENTARY

4

THE GOSPEL ACCORDING AND THE JOHANNINE EPISTLES

Neal M. Flanagan, O.S.M.

COLLEGEVILLE BIBLE COMMENTARY

General Editor: Robert J. Karris, O.F.M.

Cover: Fifth-century mosaic under the main altar of the Church of the Multiplication of the Loaves at Tabgha. Photograph by Placid Stuckenschneider, O.S.B.

ABBREVIATIONS

nesis
xodus
viticus
Numbers
Deuteronomy
oshua
udges
Ruth
1 Samuel
2 Samuel
1 Kings
2 Kings
1 Chronicles
2 Chronicles
Ezra
Nehemiah
Tobit
Judith
Esther
acc – 1 Maccabees
acc – 2 Maccabees
Job
s) – Psalm(s)
ov – Proverbs
cl – Ecclesiastes

Song – Song of Songs
Wis – Wisdom
Sir – Sirach
Isa – Isaiah
Jer – Jeremiah
Lam – Lamentations
Bar – Baruch
Ezek – Ezekiel
Dan – Daniel
Hos – Hosea
Joel – Joel
Amos – Amos
Obad – Obadiah
Jonah – Jonah
Mic – Micah
Nah – Nahum
Hab – Habakkuk
Zeph – Zephaniah
Hag – Haggai
Zech – Zechariah
Mal – Malachi
Matt – Matthew
Mark – Mark
Luke – Luke
John – John

Act
Rom
1 Co
2 Co
Gal –
Eph –
Phil –
Col – C
1 Thess
2 Thess
1 Tim – 1
2 Tim – 2
Titus – Tit
Phlm – Phi
Heb – Hebr
Jas – James
1 Pet – 1 Pet
2 Pet – 2 Pe
1 John – 1 J
2 John – 2 J
3 John – 3 J
Jude – Jude
Rev – Reve

Nihil obstat: Robert C. Harren, J.C.L., *Censor deputatus.*
Imprimatur: ✝ George H. Speltz, D.D., Bishop of St. Cloud. July 22,

e text of the New Testament from the NEW AMERICAN BIBLE, co
e Confraternity of Christian Doctrine, Washington, D.C., is reproduced
aid copyright owner. No part of the NEW AMERICAN BIBLE may be rep
without permission in writing. All rights reserved.

ISBN 0-8146-1304-7 (volume 4); ISBN 0-8146-1312-8 (11-volume

Library of Congress Cataloging in Publication Data

Flanagan, Neal M.
    The Gospel according to John and the Johannine Epistles.

    (Collegeville Bible commentary)
    Includes text of the Gospel of John and the Epistles of John
    1. Bible. N.T. John – Criticism, interpretation, etc.
John – Criticism, interpretation, etc. I. Bible. N.T. Jo
1983. II. Bible. N.T. Epistles of John. English. Ne
IV. Series.
BS2601.F55   1983   226.5077   82-22908
ISBN 0-8146-1304-7

COLLEGEVILLE BIBLE COMMENTARY

THE GOSPEL
ACCORDING T[O]
AND THE
JOHANNINE EPIS[TLES]

Neal M. Flanagan, O.S.M.

THE LITURGICAL PRESS

Collegeville, Minnesota

CONTENTS

DEDICATION
To the dearest of friends:
Christel, Johannes, Jofin, Paul

The Gospel According to John

Introduction

This introduction is not intended to be an initial, preparatory summation of John's theology nor a presentation — with solutions — of the various problems regarding the author of the Gospel and the nature of his community. I prefer that the readers first have the opportunity to study through the Fourth Gospel as a journey of discovery. Only at the end, after they have assimilated much of what John himself has to say, will I attempt to pull elements together into a résumé.

The commentary is not a verse-by-verse study, though of course numerous individual verses will be considered. Insistence will be placed, rather, on the illumination of the successive Johannine themes as our author offers them to us. The Scripture text is that of the New American Bible, but the commentary will be of use no matter which translation the reader prefers.

Scholars are by no means in agreement as to the literary divisions intended by the author. My own strong preference is for those of C. H. Dodd, who divides the material into two main sections: the Book of Signs (chs. 1–12) and the Book of Glory (chs. 13–20). The Book of Signs is subsequently divided into seven thematic episodes. It is this division that I will follow here.

With sincere thanks I admit my debt to a long list of previous and contemporary scholars, but especially to C. H. Dodd, B. Lindars, R. E. Brown, J. L. Martyn and O. Cullmann. I stand on their shoulders.

The Gospel According to John

Text and Commentary

A. THE INTRODUCTION

John 1:1-51

The first chapter of John serves as an introduction to the whole Gospel introducing the reader both to John's theology — what he believes about God and Jesus — and to Jesus' ministry. It contains a prologue and a series of testimonies.

a) 1:1-18 Prologue. The prologue serves somewhat like an overture to a formal musical composition. It may well have been written after the main body of the Gospel. (This is true of most prologues.) In its short span of eighteen verses, it states briefly what the whole of the Gospel will spell out over twenty-one chapters. It has both structure and content. The *structure* has been partially determined by the presentation of "wisdom personified" in the Old Testament books. There, as in Wis 9:9-12 or Prov 8:22-36 wisdom is first with God, then shares in creation, will come to earth, and there gift humankind. This same progression is found in our prologue. The other factor that has determined the structure is the Hebrew fondness for parallelism — notions being repeated in order — and for inverse parallelism that is, repeated in inverse order. Visually, John's poetic prologue unfolds like this:

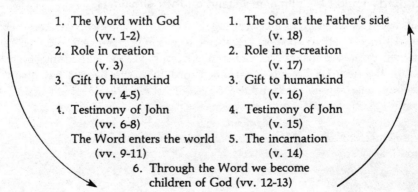

1. The Word with God (vv. 1-2)	1. The Son at the Father's side (v. 18)
2. Role in creation (v. 3)	2. Role in re-creation (v. 17)
3. Gift to humankind (vv. 4-5)	3. Gift to humankind (v. 16)
4. Testimony of John (vv. 6-8)	4. Testimony of John (v. 15)
The Word enters the world (vv. 9-11)	5. The incarnation (v. 14)
6. Through the Word we become children of God (vv. 12-13)	

I. PROLOGUE

1In the beginning was the Word;
the Word was in God's presence,
and the Word was God.
He was present to God in the beginning.
Through him all things came into being,
and apart from him nothing came to be.
Whatever came to be in him, found life,
life for the light of men.
The light shines on in darkness,
a darkness that did not overcome it.
There was a man named John sent by God, 7who came as a witness to testify to the light, so that through him all men might believe — 8but only to testify to the light, for he himself was not the light. 9The real light which gives light to every man was coming into the world.

10 He was in the world,
and through him the world was made,
yet the world did not know who he was.
11 To his own he came,
yet his own did not accept him.
12 Any who did accept him
he empowered to become children of God.

The movement of the prologue swings like the arm of a mighty pendulum, each point of which on the left side will be matched by an equivalent on the right.

In *content*, these eighteen verses speak of God's revelation, of how he has explained himself to us. It is this that accounts for the extraordinary title that our author uses — "the Word." Its best equivalent is "revelation." As we humans reveal ourselves through what we say and, even more, by what we do (our body language), so God through the centuries has offered his own self-revelation through act and speech. The prologue details this. God revealed himself through creation (vv. 2-5), but also through his Old Testament word (vv. 10-13), that is, through his covenants, the Mosaic writings, the prophets, and the wisdom literature. Those who opened their eyes and believed in this ancient revelation became "children of God . . . begotten . . by God (vv. 12-13). Finally God has revealed himself to the utmost through the incarnation of the Word, in whom God's glory, his presence, stands revealed as a sign of his enduring love (v. 14). (The Greek text tells us that the Word "pitched his tent" among us, a striking reference to God's Old Testament presence in the tent-tabernacle during Moses' wanderings with Israel in the desert.) To this incarnate Word John the Baptist has given testimony, a testimony that initiated the historical manifestation of Jesus, in whom the Father stands completely revealed and in whose fullness we, the Christian community, have all shared. The prologue ends with the upstroke of the pendulum arm to the right, in parallel to the very beginning of the poem. The Word, whose name is Jesus Christ (v. 17), is the Son, the only one, who stands "at the Father's side" (v. 18) and reveals him to those open to light and truth.

These are they who believe in his name —¹³who were begotten not by blood, nor by carnal desire, nor by man's willing it, but by God.

¹⁴ The Word became flesh
and made his dwelling among us,
and we have seen his glory:
The glory of an only Son coming
   from the Father,
filled with enduring love.

¹⁵John testified to him by proclaiming: 'This is he of whom I said, 'The one who comes after me ranks ahead of me, for he was before me.'"

¹⁶ Of his fullness
we have all had a share —
love following upon love.

¹⁷For while the law was given through Moses, this enduring love came through Jesus Christ. ¹⁸No one has ever seen God. It is God the only Son, ever at the Father's side, who has revealed him.

II. THE BOOK OF SIGNS

Testimony of John to the Envoy
¹⁹The testimony John gave when th Jews sent priests and Levites from Jeru salem to ask, "Who are you?" ²⁰was th direct statement, "I am not the Messiah ²¹They questioned him further, "Who then? Elijah?" "I am not Elijah," h answered. "Are you the Prophet?" "No he replied.

²²Finally they said to him: "Tell u who you are, so that we can give som answer to those who sent us. What d you have to say for yourself?" ²³He said quoting the prophet Isaiah, "I am

'a voice in the desert, crying out:
Make straight the way of the Lord!'

²⁴Those whom the Pharisees had ser ²⁵proceeded to question him further: " you are not the Messiah, nor Elijah, nc the Prophet, why do you baptize' ²⁶John answered them: "I baptize wit

As you may have noticed, this explanation of the content of the pro logue has ignored verses 6-8, the initial statement about John the Baptist and in so doing has been able to interpret verses 9-13 as pre-incarnationa that is, as referring to the Old Testament revelation rather than to th historical presence of Jesus in the world. In our opinion, verses 6-8 occu where they do simply to balance the statement about the Baptist on the righ side of the pendulum swing (v. 15). They are where they are, not for theo logical sequence, but for purely artistic reasons.

Consequently, verses 1-18 are an artistically fashioned poem summari ing the main point of John's theology: Jesus of Nazareth is God's suprem revelation, God's interpreter, his exegete. Being God himself (vv. 1, 18), h not only mediates God to us, he *immediates* him. He is God's wisdor speaking God's ultimate word about himself.

b) 1:19-51 Testimonies. This second section of chapter 1 contains whole list of witnesses to Jesus who, one by one, identify Jesus for John's au dience. Like the audience at a play, who by means of the printed progra: receive advance information about the actors, so these verses in John pu the readers/hearers in a position of special knowledge as the drama of Jesu life-story is played out. From the very beginning they are told who an what Jesus is. In diagram form the testimonies flow as follows:

water. There is one among you whom you do not recognize — [27]the one who is to come after me — the strap of whose sandal I am not worthy to unfasten."

[28]This happened in Bethany, across the Jordan, where John was baptizing. **His Testimony to Jesus.** [29]The next day, when John caught sight of Jesus coming toward him, he exclaimed:

"Look! There is the Lamb of God who takes away the sin of the world!

[30]It is he of whom I said:

'After me is to come a man who ranks ahead of me, because he was before me.'

[31]I confess I did not recognize him, though the very reason I came baptizing with water was that he might be revealed to Israel."

[32]John gave this testimony also:

"I saw the Spirit descend like a dove from the sky, and it came to rest on him.

[33]But I did not recognize him. The one who sent me to baptize with water told me, 'When you see the Spirit descend and rest on someone, it is he who is to baptize with the Holy Spirit.' [34]Now I have seen for myself and have testified, 'This is God's chosen One.'"

The First Disciples. [35]The next day John was there again with two of his disciples. [36]As he watched Jesus walk by he said, "Look! There is the Lamb of God!" [37]The two disciples heard what he

DAY	WITNESS	TESTIMONY
1st (vv. 19-28)	John the Baptist to priests and Levites	John is not Christ, nor the expected Elijah of Mal 3:23 (4:5 in some versions), nor the prophet of Deut 18:15, 18, but "a voice in the desert," himself unworthy to untie the sandal strap of the one coming after him.
2nd ("next day" of vv. 29-34)	John the Baptist at sight of Jesus	Jesus is "the Lamb of God who takes away the sin of the world"; he who ranks before John; he on whom the Spirit descended and who baptizes with the Spirit; God's chosen One.
3rd ("next day" of vv. 35-39)	John the Baptist to two of his disciples, who go to Jesus about 4 p.m. and stay	"Look! There is the Lamb of God!" (This would be a reference to the paschal lamb and/or to the suffering servant of Isa 53:7, silent before its shearers.)

said, and followed Jesus. ³⁸When Jesus turned around and noticed them following him, he asked them, "What are you looking for?" They said to him, "Rabbi (which means Teacher), where do you stay?" ³⁹"Come and see," he answered. So they went to see where he was lodged, and stayed with him that day. (It was about four in the afternoon.) ⁴⁰One of the two who had followed him after hearing John was Simon Peter's brother Andrew. ⁴¹The first thing he did was seek out his brother Simon and tell him, "We have found the Messiah!" (This term means the Anointed.) ⁴²He brought him to Jesus, who looked at him and said, "You are Simon, son of John; your name shall be Cephas (which is rendered Peter)."

⁴³The next day he wanted to set out for Galilee, but first he came upon Philip. "Follow me," Jesus said to him. ⁴⁴Now Philip was from Bethsaida, the same town as Andrew and Peter.

⁴⁵Philip sought out Nathanael and told him, "We have found the one Moses spoke of in the law—the prophets too—Jesus, son of Joseph, from Nazareth." ⁴⁶Nathanael's response to that was, "Can anything good come from Nazareth?" and Philip replied, "Come, see for yourself." ⁴⁷When Jesus saw Nathanael coming toward him, he remarked: "This man is a true Israelite. There is no guile in him." ⁴⁸"How do you know me?" Nathanael asked him. "Before Philip called you," Jesus answered, "I saw you under the fig tree." ⁴⁹"Rabbi," said Nathanael, "you are the Son of God; you are the king of Israel." ⁵⁰Jesus responded: "Do you believe just because I told you I saw you under the fig tree? You will see much greater things than that."

⁵¹He went on to tell them, "I solemnly assure you, you shall see the sky opened and the angels of God ascending and descending on the Son of Man."

4th(?) (vv. 40-42)	Andrew to Simon	"We have found the Messiah."
5th ("next day" of vv. 43-51)	Philip to Nathaniel	"the one Moses spoke of in the law—the prophets too."
	Nathaniel	"You are the Son of God; you are the king of Israel."
7th ("On the third day" of 2:1-11)	Jesus' Cana miracle	"Thus did he reveal his glory, and his disciples believed in him" (2:11).

Our author seems to be laying out an artistic first week in the good news of Christian re-creation to recall the first week of the creation story in the Book of Genesis. Both Genesis and John's Gospel begin with the identical phrase, "In the beginning." This is probably intentional. The succession of days in John are clearly marked except for the fourth, where the otherwise unnecessary reference to the two disciples going to Jesus about 4 p.m. and staying with him (v. 39) intends to say that they stayed overnight. Why else would John mention 4 p.m.? This first week of re-creation will conclude with the Cana miracle and the first manifestation that in Jesus is God's

THE GOSPEL ACCORDING TO JOHN

AND THE

JOHANNINE EPISTLES

Neal M. Flanagan, O.S.M.

THE LITURGICAL PRESS

Collegeville, Minnesota

ABBREVIATIONS

Gen — Genesis
Exod — Exodus
Lev — Leviticus
Num — Numbers
Deut — Deuteronomy
Josh — Joshua
Judg — Judges
Ruth — Ruth
1 Sam — 1 Samuel
2 Sam — 2 Samuel
1 Kgs — 1 Kings
2 Kgs — 2 Kings
1 Chr — 1 Chronicles
2 Chr — 2 Chronicles
Ezra — Ezra
Neh — Nehemiah
Tob — Tobit
Jdt — Judith
Esth — Esther
1 Macc — 1 Maccabees
2 Macc — 2 Maccabees
Job — Job
Ps(s) — Psalm(s)
Prov — Proverbs
Eccl — Ecclesiastes

Song — Song of Songs
Wis — Wisdom
Sir — Sirach
Isa — Isaiah
Jer — Jeremiah
Lam — Lamentations
Bar — Baruch
Ezek — Ezekiel
Dan — Daniel
Hos — Hosea
Joel — Joel
Amos — Amos
Obad — Obadiah
Jonah — Jonah
Mic — Micah
Nah — Nahum
Hab — Habakkuk
Zeph — Zephaniah
Hag — Haggai
Zech — Zechariah
Mal — Malachi
Matt — Matthew
Mark — Mark
Luke — Luke
John — John

Acts — Acts
Rom — Romans
1 Cor — 1 Corinthians
2 Cor — 2 Corinthians
Gal — Galatians
Eph — Ephesians
Phil — Philippians
Col — Colossians
1 Thess — 1 Thessalonian
2 Thess — 2 Thessalonian
1 Tim — 1 Timothy
2 Tim — 2 Timothy
Titus — Titus
Phlm — Philemon
Heb — Hebrews
Jas — James
1 Pet — 1 Peter
2 Pet — 2 Peter
1 John — 1 John
2 John — 2 John
3 John — 3 John
Jude — Jude
Rev — Revelation

Nihil obstat: Robert C. Harren, J.C.L., *Censor deputatus.*

Imprimatur: ✠ George H. Speltz, D.D., Bishop of St. Cloud. July 22, 1982.

ISBN 0-8146-1304-7 (volume 4); ISBN 0-8146-1312-8 (11-volume set)

Library of Congress Cataloging in Publication Data

Flanagan, Neal M.

The Gospel according to John and the Johannine Epistles.

(Collegeville Bible commentary)

Includes text of the Gospel of John and the Epistles of John from the New American Bible

1. Bible. N.T. John — Criticism, interpretation, etc. 2. Bible. N.T. Epistles c John — Criticism, interpretation, etc. I. Bible. N.T. John. English. New American 1983. II. Bible. N.T. Epistles of John. English. New American. 1983. III. Title IV. Series.

BS2601.F55   1983   226.5077   82-22908

ISBN 0-8146-1304-7

:esiding glory, his divine presence. "On the third day" of 2:1 should also re-
nind us of *the* future supreme manifestation of God's glory, the resurrec-
ion.

This series of testimonies can be a source of confusion and difficulty for
anyone who has read Mark's Gospel, in which the disciples come to their
aith-knowledge of Jesus only hesitantly, timidly, and imperfectly—and
:hat over a lengthy period of time. John seems to contradict Mark's picture.
By the end of chapter 1 the Johannine disciples seem to know everything
:here is to know about Jesus, even his divinity. I think we must say that
Iohn is not attempting here to give a historical presentation of the first
disciples' advance in faith. He has a different purpose in mind. He wishes to
mpress these christological statements on the minds of his audience at the
very start of his dramatic presentation; therefore his actors appear in a suc-
:ession of brief scenes to pass along the required information. The testimonies indicate that the Gospel's main interest is Christology. John may
also wish to indicate through this procedure the way in which his own community advanced to its knowledge of Jesus: by moving from the circle of
Iohn the Baptist to the greater personage of Jesus, who was gradually recognized as the Lamb of God, God's chosen One, the Messiah, Son of God, and
King of Israel. Jesus was the fulfillment of all the Old Testament hopes.

There is another purpose that John, a man of rich creative genius, may
have intended. His list of characters in this first act/period of seven days
seems to typify the basic personal elements of the Christian community. In
order there appear: (1) John the Baptist, precursor to the new creation,
whose sole function is to witness; (2) the Savior; (3) disciples who hear,
follow, look for, and stay; (4) Peter, the rock; (5) missionaries like Andrew
and Philip who spread the good news; (6) Nathaniel, the true Israelite in
whom there is no guile, who, as some Jewish traditions expressed it, studied
law under a fig tree and was rewarded. With this, the founding elements of
the community are assembled. Let the drama begin!

The unexpected and ambiguous reference in verse 51 to a future vision
of angels "ascending and descending on the Son of Man" insinuates the unifying function of Jesus. Like the angels on Jacob's ladder (Gen 28:12), he will
join through himself the above and the below, the heavenly and the earthly.

2 **The Wedding at Cana.** ¹On the third day there was a wedding at Cana in Galilee, and the mother of Jesus was there. ²Jesus and his disciples had likewise been invited to the celebration. ³At a certain point the wine ran out, and Jesus' mother told him, "They have no more wine." ⁴Jesus replied, "Woman, how does this concern of yours involve me? My hour has not yet come." ⁵His mother instructed those waiting on table, "Do whatever he tells you." ⁶As prescribed for Jewish ceremonial washings, there were at hand six stone water jars, each one holding fifteen to twenty-five gallons. ⁷"Fill those jars with water," Jesus ordered, at which they filled them to the brim. ⁸"Now," he said, "draw some out and take it to the waiter in charge." They did as he instructed them. ⁹The waiter in charge tasted the water made wine, without knowing

B. THE BOOK OF SIGNS

John 2:1–12:50

Our author begins at this point what is aptly called "The Book of Signs." It moves by way of narrative and discourse through seven distinguishable episodes, or themes, and through seven sign-miracles. John's terminology regarding these sign-miracles is very distinct: they are "signs" pointing to some deeper theological truth. What the deeper truth is will frequently, but not always, be identified in the discourse. The material in these eleven chapters appears to be organized into theme clusters, which we will call "episodes."

2:1–4:42 Episode I: New Beginnings

In this section John will provide four different accounts—Cana, the temple, Nicodemus, the Samaritan woman—each of which will emphasize the newness that Jesus has brought into the world. The basic message throughout will be the same as that of Paul in 2 Cor 5:17: "The old order has passed away; now all is new!" John's Gospel is in many ways a Christian Genesis, a story of re-creation.

1. The Cana sign (2:1-12). With this account, located in the small town of Cana, north in Galilee, John begins his sign theology: "Jesus performed this first of his signs" (v. 11). The question, as always in John, is: What does the sign mean? In this instance the meaning is multiple, but it is centered on one basic point: the arrival through Jesus of the new messianic age. What is changed in this incident is not simply water, but water for Old Testament ceremonial washings. It is changed not simply into wine, but into wine of highest quality and of surprising quantity (six jars, each holding fifteen to twenty-five gallons). Such a superabundance of wine was a frequent prophetic figure of speech for the dawning of the messianic age (Amos 9:13-14; Joel 3:18). The symbol was current also at the time of Jesus, as we read in

where it had come from; only the waiters knew, since they had drawn the water. Then the waiter in charge called the groom over [10]and remarked to him: People usually serve the choice wine first; then when the guests have been drinking awhile, a lesser vintage. What you have done is keep the choice wine until now." [11]Jesus performed this first of his signs at Cana in Galilee. Thus did he reveal his glory, and his disciples believed in him.

[12]After this he went down to Capernaum, along with his mother and brothers [and his disciples] but they stayed there only a few days.

the almost contemporary 2 Baruch 29: ". . . on each vine there shall be a thousand branches, and each branch shall bear a thousand clusters, and each cluster produce a thousand grapes, and each grape produce a cor about 120 gallons] of wine . . . because these are they who have come to the consummation of time."

Changing Old Testament water into messianic wine, consequently, signifies, or signs, for John the passing of the old into the new. The messianic era has arrived. The feast symbolizes the messianic banquet. And the messianic bridegroom, he who supplies the wine, is Jesus himself (3:29). The allusion to the hour of Jesus' death in verse 4 may even mean that John wants his audience to think also of the messianic wine that will be the result and Eucharistic sacrament of Jesus' death.

Verse 4, "Woman, how does this concern of yours involve me? My hour has not yet come," is extremely difficult to explain. Cancel the verse out and the story flows with ease. Leave it in, as the text itself demands, and we have the mother asking, Jesus responding negatively, yet the sign-miracle taking place. Leave it in, and we must ask: Why does Jesus call his mother "Woman"? Why is his verbal response negative but his action positive? Of what "hour" does Jesus speak? Explanations of all this are multiple and extremely divergent. One of the most probable is that verse 4 was not in the original pre-Gospel account, which presented a straightforward story of the incident in which the mother's request was answered by the son's positive response. The evangelist, however, who wished to use the story for his theme of new beginnings, inserted verse 4 to affirm, as do the other Gospels, that during Jesus' public life, until his hour came, his work was determined solely by the Father's will. It is this which is stated by the negative tone of the response and by the use of the impersonal "Woman."

John has also used this story to initiate his theology of glory. "Thus did he reveal his glory" (v. 11). This is the beginning of a magnificent Johannine conception of glory as being *God's manifested presence*. God glorifies us when he manifests himself in us; we glorify him when we manifest him to the world. In this instance at Cana, God's presence is manifested in his Son, his Revealer.

Cleansing of the Temple. [13]As the Jewish Passover was near, Jesus went up to Jerusalem. [14]In the temple precincts he came upon people engaged in selling oxen, sheep and doves, and others seated changing coins. [15]He made a [kind of] whip of cords and drove sheep and oxen alike out of the temple area, and knocked over the money-changers' tables, spilling their coins. [16]He told those who were selling doves: "Get them out of here! Stop turning my Father's house into a market-place!" [17]His disciples recalled the words of Scripture "Zeal for your house consumes me." [18]At this the Jews responded, "What sign can you show us authorizing you to do these things?" [19]"Destroy this temple,"

2. The temple purification (2:13-25). This is another newness or transformation story. The temple itself will be replaced. Destroyed in A.D 70 by the soldiers of Titus' Roman army, its place as the center of worship and sacrifice, the site of God's presence and the visible symbol of his fidelity, will be taken by the risen body of Christ. The physical destruction of the temple was a spirit-crushing disaster for Israel. The loss was softened for Jewish Christians by this Johannine theology of the Christ-temple, which, indeed, Paul had already expanded into a doctrine of the Christian-temple (1 Cor 6:19).

This physical purification of the temple might remind us of the type of symbolic deeds acted out by the prophets; and, indeed, Jesus' approach to the temple on this occasion resembles that of Jeremiah (Jer 7). The action, though not a miracle, is a sign, a double sign. The temple, soon to be destroyed, stood in need of purification. And its function would be replaced by the risen body of Christ.

Jesus goes up to Jerusalem at Passover time (v. 13) at the beginning of his ministry. This stands in contrast to the other Gospels, in which Jesus goes to Jerusalem but once, and then at the very end of his ministry. With regard to multiple visits, John is probably more correct historically. Our author has considerably more interest in Jerusalem than the other evangelists, an indication that his roots are more oriented in Jerusalem than in Galilee. The temple purification, however, probably occurred toward the end of Jesus' life, as the Synoptists (Matthew, Mark, Luke) indicate, serving as a final straw leading to Jesus' condemnation. John may well have transferred the story to this initial phase in Jesus' life because it fits so well into his "newness" theme and because he intends that Lazarus' resurrection (ch. 11) be the incident leading to the crucifixion (11:53; 12:10).

The mention of "forty-six years" in verse 20 is one of the clearest chronological indications given in the Gospels (see Luke 3:1 for another). This temple, which was finished in the early sixties, was begun by Herod in 20–19 B.C. The addition of John's forty-six years would date this scene to about A.D. 28.

was Jesus' answer, "and in three days I will raise it up." ²⁰They retorted, "This temple took forty-six years to build, and you are going to 'raise it up in three days'!" ²¹Actually he was talking about the temple of his body. ²²Only after Jesus had been raised from the dead did his disciples recall that he had said this, and come to believe the Scripture and the word he had spoken.

²³While he was in Jerusalem during the Passover festival, many believed in his name, for they could see the signs he was performing. ²⁴For his part, Jesus would not trust himself to them because he knew them all. ²⁵He needed no one to give him testimony about human nature. He was well aware of what was in man's heart.

3 **Nicodemus.** ¹A certain Pharisee named Nicodemus, a member of the Jewish Sanhedrin, ²came to him at night. "Rabbi," he said, "we know you are a teacher come from God, for no man can perform signs and wonders such as you perform unless God is with him." ³Jesus gave him this answer:

"I solemnly assure you,
no one can see the reign of God
unless he is begotten from above."

Finally, there are four Johannine peculiarities that make their first appearance in this incident:

a) "The Jews" appear (v. 18) as the primary antagonists of Jesus. Certainly Jesus the Jew and his Jewish disciples had their share of difficulties with their Jewish contemporaries; but the marked distinction between Jesus and Jews must echo the later and sharper antagonism between Jews and Christians during the period of John's own community.

b) We find in verses 19-21 the first appearance of a dramatic technique by which the author makes his point through a progression from ambiguity to misunderstanding to comprehension. The ambiguity of verse 19 leads to the misunderstanding of verse 20 and to the final clarification of verse 21. This technique will occur frequently in the Gospel.

c) Verse 22 tells us that many of Jesus' words and acts were not understood during his lifetime but became intelligible only through the light of his resurrection. It is from this perspective that our evangelist writes.

d) Finally, in verse 23, John speaks of the many who believed because they could see the signs Jesus performed. We must be cautious here. John is not speaking of a deep and viable faith in this and the following verses; he is speaking of the initial faith of those who simply see the signs. It is not those who see that become the true disciples but those who understand. In the incident that follows we shall see a man attracted by signs (3:2) but with little understanding of what they mean.

3. Nicodemus (3:1-36). As a further development of the theme of "newness," John brings Nicodemus onto the scene, but in the night darkness that symbolizes lack of faith-light. Nicodemus has been attracted by Jesus' signs, an attraction not to be despised, yet at a distance from true faith. He has a role to play in the drama, for he is both a Jewish leader (v. 1) and a teacher

⁴"How can a man be born again once he is old?" retorted Nicodemus. "Can he return to his mother's womb and be born over again?" ⁵Jesus replied:

"I solemnly assure you,
no one can enter into God's kingdom
without being begotten of water and Spirit.
⁶ Flesh begets flesh,
Spirit begets spirit.
⁷ Do not be surprised that I tell you
you must all be begotten from above.
⁸ The wind blows where it will.
You hear the sound it makes
but you do not know where it comes from,
or where it goes.
So it is with everyone begotten of the Spirit."

⁹"How can such a thing happen?" asked Nicodemus. ¹⁰Jesus responded: "You hold the office of teacher of Israel and still you do not understand these matters?
¹¹ "I solemnly assure you,
we are talking about what we know,
we are testifying to what we have seen,
but you do not accept our testimony.
¹² If you do not believe
when I tell you about earthly things,

of Israel (v. 10), a representative of so many interested Jews over the decades after Christ who have shown initial interest in Jesus. A dialogue ensues, animated once more by ambiguity and misunderstanding. Entrance into the "kingdom" (this expression is limited to vv. 3-5 in John, who prefers rather to speak of "life" or "eternal life") depends on being reborn through water and Spirit. Verse 3 speaks of birth "from above." The original Greek at this point can mean either "from above" or "again." John is quite capable of meaning both, though his future statement in verse 31 should incline us to put the greater emphasis on "from above." The "wind" of verse 8 might seem to introduce a jarring notion, but the Greek for "wind" and "spirit" is the same, *pneuma*; and our text is saying that the origin and movement of both wind and spirit is a divine mystery.

What begins as a dialogue in verses 1-10 turns into a monologue in verses 11-12 as Nicodemus disappears momentarily into the darkness from which he came. (He will reappear in better light in 7:50-52 and for a courageous action of discipleship in 19:39-42.) This pattern of dialogue turning to monologue is frequent in the Fourth Gospel, where minor characters are at times introduced simply to help develop an important theme. The Greek original is interesting at this juncture as singulars change into plurals, and Jesus addresses not simply Nicodemus but a world of Nicodemuses as well as John's readers and hearers. Thus verses 11-12 read in Greek: "I solemnly assure you (singular) . . . but you (plural) do not accept our testimony. If you (plural) do not believe when I tell you (plural) about earthly things, how are you (plural) to believe when I tell you (plural) about those of heaven?"

how are you to believe
when I tell you about those of
heaven?

13 No one has gone up to heaven
except the One who came down
from there —
the Son of Man [who is in heaven].

14 Just as Moses lifted up the serpent
in the desert,
so must the Son of Man be lifted
up,

15 that all who believe
may have eternal life in him.

16 Yes, God so loved the world
that he gave his only Son,
that whoever believes in him may
not die
but may have eternal life.

17 God did not send the Son into the
world
to condemn the world,
but that the world might be saved
through him.

18 Whoever believes in him avoids
condemnation,
but whoever does not believe is
already condemned
for not believing in the name of
God's only Son.

19 The judgment of condemnation is
this:
the light came into the world,
but men loved darkness rather
than light
because their deeds were wicked.

20 Everyone who practices evil
hates the light;
he does not come near it
for fear his deeds will be exposed.

21 But he who acts in truth
comes into the light,
to make clear
that his deeds are done in God."

Verse 14 contains both an allusion to an Old Testament incident and the introduction of important Johannine theology. The elevated serpent in the desert refers to a fairly confusing incident in Num 21:9 in which a bronze serpent raised on a pole by Moses was a source of salvation (Wis 16:6). To this reference John adds that the Son of Man, too, "must be lifted up." This phrasing will be repeated three more times (8:28; 12:32, 34), and its theology of crucifixion-exaltation will be clarified as the Gospel proceeds.

Extremely important for Johannine and Christian theology is the conviction that God's love (v. 16) is the dynamic principle for world salvation. Jesus' God, John's God, our God is a God motivated by love so great that he has gifted the world with his own Son, not to condemn but to save.

John uses the word "world" (v. 17) in different senses. Here its use is neutral. The whole of creation, and in particular its human inhabitants, is the object of God's saving love. More frequently, as we shall see, "the world" will become symbolic for those who refuse to believe. It is mainly of these that verses 18-21 speak. Though Jesus has come to save and not to condemn, human actions play their own part in determining salvation and condemnation. Salvation is belief in Jesus (v. 18) accompanied by deeds done in God (v. 21). Condemnation is a from-within process, consisting in non-belief in the light that is Jesus, accompanied by the evil works done in the darkness. The light-darkness opposition should remind us of the same theme in the prologue (1:4-5).

17

Final Witness of the Baptizer. ²²Later on, Jesus and his disciples came into Judean territory, and he spent some time with them there baptizing. ²³John too was baptizing at Aenon near Salim where water was plentiful, and people kept coming to be baptized. ²⁴(John, of course, had not yet been thrown into prison.) ²⁵A controversy about purification arose between John's disciples and a certain Jew. ²⁶So they came to John, saying, "Rabbi, the man who was with you across the Jordan—the one about whom you have been testifying—is baptizing now, and everyone is flocking to him." ²⁷John answered:

"No one can lay hold on anything
unless it is given him from on high.

²⁸You yourselves are witnesses to the fact that I said: 'I am not the Messiah; I am sent before him.'

²⁹ "It is the groom who has the bride.
The groom's best man
waits there listening for him
and is overjoyed to hear his voice.
That is my joy, and it is complete.
³⁰ He must increase,
while I must decrease.

Discourse Concluded

³¹ "The One who comes from above is
above all;
the one who is of the earth is earthly,
and he speaks on an earthly plane.
The One who comes from heaven
[who is above all]
³² testifies to what he has seen and
heard,
but no one accepts his testimony.
³³ Whoever does accept this testimony
certifies that God is truthful.
³⁴ For the One whom God has sent
speaks the words of God;

Verses 22-30 present the Baptist's final witness to Jesus. They constitute such an obvious break between the preceding verses and those that follow (vv. 31-36) that many scholars believe they are out of place here. This need not be. John may have wanted to reintroduce the Baptist here to clarify through baptismal references what was meant by "begotten of *water and Spirit*" in verse 5. This reintroduction is admittedly awkward, but it might well serve this purpose. John's baptism (the site of Aenon near Salim in verse 23 is uncertain) leads into Jesus' form of baptism, the type suggested by verse 5. John's last testimony is given in verses 27-30. Here, as in 1:19-36, the Baptist stresses Jesus' superiority. (This stressing may flow from the fact that John's own community had opposition from descendants of the Baptist's original followers who claimed that the Baptist, not Jesus, was the real Messiah.) "He must increase, while I must decrease," says the Baptist (v. 30). And with these apt words he disappears personally from the Gospel.

What follows in verses 31-36 seems to be a continuation of verse 21, interrupted by the paragraph concerning the Baptist. There is a sharp distinction in this Gospel between above and below, light and darkness, belief and unbelief—and all of this centers upon the person of Jesus who comes from above (v. 31) and testifies to what he has seen (v. 32) as the One whom God has sent (v. 34). To believe in Jesus is to accept the Father and the Father's love, to have and live eternal life. The content of the final verse, "Whoever believes in the Son has life eternal," both summarizes the whole of the

he does not ration his gift of the
Spirit.
*⁵ The Father loves the Son
and has given everything over to
him.
*⁶ Whoever believes in the Son
has life eternal.
Whoever disobeys the Son
will not see life,
but must endure the wrath of God."

4 ¹Now when Jesus learned that the
Pharisees had heard that he was win-
ning over and baptizing more disciples
than John ²(in fact, however, it was not
Jesus himself who baptized, but his disciples), ³he left Judea and started back
for Galilee again.
The Samaritan Woman. ⁴He had to
pass through Samaria, ⁵and his journey
brought him to a Samaritan town named

chapter and ties the chapter's ending to identical statements in its centrally
located verses 15-16. The "wrath of God" (v. 36) is the loss of life, the death
and darkness that are willful unbelief.

4. The Samaritan woman (4:1-42). The evangelist has already presented
us with various aspects of the "newness" that Jesus brings. It is the messianic
wine of Cana, abundant and exquisite; the renovated temple of God; a
rebirth in water and Spirit. In this next attempt to describe God's gift in
Christ, John pictures it as *a spring of fresh water*, life-giving, welling up into
eternal life; as *a worship suitable to God who is Spirit*, a worship therefore
in the Spirit of truth. He insists, moreover, that Jesus' food is the accom-
plishment of his Father's will. Part of that will is the missionary work in
fields ripe for harvest.

This chapter is surely one of the most dramatically constructed in the
Gospel. Divide it into its various speaking parts—(1) a narrator; (2) Jesus;
(3) the Samaritan woman; (4) the disciples; (5) the townsfolk—and you
have instant theater. Another element in the account that lends itself to
dramatic presentation is the way the stage is cleared for dialogue with the
woman by the disciples' departure (v. 8), and for dialogue with the disciples
by the woman's exit (v. 28). Her jar, left behind in verse 28, acts like a stage
prop to advise the audience that she will return. There is even dramatic progression in the faith-knowledge of the woman and her townsfolk. From simple knowledge that Jesus is a Jew (v. 9), the characters move to belief in him
as prophet (v. 19), Christ (vv. 25-26, 29) and, finally, Savior of the world
(v. 42).

The chapter, additionally, is excellently structured, focusing on the two
central dialogues—the first with the woman, the second with the disciples.
The structure is built like this:

> *Introduction* (vv. 1-6), in which Jesus leaves Judea for Galilee to the
> north. Enroute he passes through Samaria, where, at Shechem, he rests
> at noon next to Jacob's well (still in useful existence today).

Shechem near the plot of land which Jacob had given to his son Joseph. 6This was the site of Jacob's well. Jesus, tired from his journey, sat down at the well.

The hour was about noon. 7When a Samaritan woman came to draw water, Jesus said to her, "Give me a drink." 8(His disciples had gone off to the town to buy provisions.) 9The Samaritan woman said to him, "You are a Jew. How can you ask me, a Samaritan and a woman, for a drink?" (Recall that Jews have nothing to do with Samaritans.) 10Jesus replied:

"If only you recognized God's gift,
and who it is that is asking you for a drink,
you would have asked him instead,
and he would have given you living water."

11"Sir," she challenged him, "you do not have a bucket and this well is deep. Where do you expect to get this flowing water? 12Surely you do not pretend to be greater than our ancestor Jacob, who gave us this well and drank from it with his sons and his flocks?" 13Jesus replied:

"Everyone who drinks this water
will be thirsty again.
14 But whoever drinks the water I give him
will never be thirsty;

no, the water I give
shall become a fountain within him
leaping up to provide eternal life."

15The woman said to him, "Give me this water, sir, so that I shall not grow thirsty and have to keep coming here to draw water."

16He said to her, "Go, call your husband, and then come back here." 17"I have no husband," replied the woman. "You are right in saying you have no husband!" Jesus exclaimed. 18"The fact is, you have had five, and the man you are living with now is not your husband. What you said is true."

19"Sir," answered the woman, "I can see you are a prophet. 20Our ancestors worshiped on this mountain, but you people claim that Jerusalem is the place where men ought to worship God." 21Jesus told her:

"Believe me, woman,
an hour is coming
when you will worship the Father
neither on this mountain
nor in Jerusalem.
22 You people worship what you do not understand,
while we understand what we worship;
after all, salvation is from the Jews.
23 Yet an hour is coming, and is already here,

FIRST DIALOGUE (vv. 7-26), between Jesus and the Samaritan woman concerning:

a) *living water* (vv. 7-15). The water of Jacob's well is surpassed by the water that Jesus will give, "a fountain . . . leaping up to provide eternal life" (v. 14).

Transition: Jesus' knowledge of the woman's past moves her toward faith: "Sir, I can see you are a prophet" (v. 19).

b) *worship in Spirit and truth* (vv. 20-26). "Yet an hour is coming, and is already here, when authentic worshipers will worship the Father in Spirit and truth" (v. 23).

The woman begins to think in terms of the Messiah. Jesus states that it is he.

when authentic worshipers
will worship the Father in Spirit and
truth.
Indeed, it is just such worshipers
the Father seeks.
24 God is Spirit,
and those who worship him
must worship in Spirit and truth."
25The woman said to him: "I know there
is a Messiah coming. (This term means
Anointed.) When he comes, he will tell
us everything." 26Jesus replied, "I who
speak to you am he."
27His disciples, returning at this point,
were surprised that Jesus was speaking
with a woman. No one put a question,
however, such as "What do you want of
him?" or "Why are you talking with
her?" 28The woman then left her water
jar and went off into the town. She said
to the people: 29"Come and see someone
who told me everything I ever did!
Could this not be the Messiah?" 30At that
they set out from the town to meet him.
31Meanwhile the disciples were urging
him, "Rabbi, eat something." 32But he
told them:
"I have food to eat
of which you do not know."
33At this the disciples said to one
another, "Do you suppose that someone
has brought him something to eat?"
34Jesus explained to them:

"Doing the will of him who sent me
and bringing his work to completion is my food.
35 Do you not have a saying:
'Four months more
and it will be harvest!'?
Listen to what I say:
Open your eyes and see!
The fields are shining for harvest!
36 The reaper already collects his
wages
and gathers a yield for eternal life,
that sower and reaper may rejoice
together.
37 Here we have the saying verified:
'One man sows; another reaps.'
38 I sent you to reap
what you had not worked for.
Others have done the labor,
and you have come into their gain."
39Many Samaritans from that town
believed in him on the strength of the
woman's word of testimony: "He told
me everything I ever did." 40The result
was that, when these Samaritans came
to him, they begged him to stay with
them awhile. So he stayed there two
days, 41and through his own spoken
word many more came to faith. 42As
they told the woman: "No longer does
our faith depend on your story. We
have heard for ourselves, and we know
that this really is the Savior of the
world."

SECOND DIALOGUE (vv. 31-38), between Jesus and the disciples concerning:
   a) *Jesus' food* (vv. 31-34). "Doing the will of him who sent me and
      bringing his work to completion is my food" (v. 34).
   b) *the harvest* (vv. 35-38). "Open your eyes and see! The fields are
      shining for harvest!" (v. 35).

Conclusion (vv. 39-42). Belief of the Samaritans: ". . . we know that
this really is the Savior of the world" (v. 42).

A few additional comments seem necessary to clarify even further the
content of this moving chapter.

1. Jewish relationship with the Samaritans lodged between Galilee to the north and Judea to the south was bad, deep, and historically conditioned. About the year 722 B.C. the Assyrian army descended upon northern Israel with force, took its populace into an exile from which it never returned, and colonized its land with foreigners who partially adopted Israel's religion over the centuries but were always viewed by the Jews as hated, semi-pagan invaders. (2 Kgs 17:23-41 gives a brief summary of the story.) The woman, therefore, was justly surprised when the Jew Jesus spoke to her and indicated that he was even willing to drink from her water jar.

2. Jesus is described in very human terms in verse 6, sitting at the well, exhausted from his journey. John usually paints his portrait of Jesus in colors more definitely divine. The woman, too, is very human. Her appearance at the well about noon (v. 6), long after the village women would have replenished their water supply for the day, may indicate her isolated position in the town's society. Sexually immoral, she was left to herself and her merry-go-round retinue of men friends. Yet it is she who, rebounding from Jesus' healing words, becomes a missionary to her people. The Lord's word moves her from isolation to faith to mission.

3. The account, as happens frequently in John, may be telescoping different periods of time. It seems to reflect strongly the Church's post-resurrection mission to Samaria, such as is described in the work of Philip, Peter, and John in Acts 8:4-25. It may even be indicative of the life-story of John's community, which would then have included, and been influenced by, Samaritan converts. What I am proposing here is that John's literary technique has rather amazing depths and turns. He specializes in bi-level presentations. There are *theological bi-levels* when, as one out of many examples, the water changed into wine (ch. 2) really speaks of the old covenant giving way to the new. Both levels are present in the Cana story; both are intended by the author. And, in a way unexpected by us twentieth-century readers, there are also *historical bi-levels*. Events in Jesus' lifetime are interpenetrated by later events happening in the life of John's community. In this chapter, water symbolizes the eternal life given by the Spirit of truth, the theological bi-level. On the other hand, the encounter with the Samaritan woman is influenced by the later, post-resurrection outreach to the Samaritans, the historical bi-level.

4. Finally, it is important to note that the conversion of the Samaritans is effected, not by any miraculous sign, but by *the force of Jesus' word*: ". . . *through his own spoken word* many more came to faith. . . . We have *heard* for ourselves, and we know that this really is the Savior of the world" (vv. 41-42). It is to this theme of the life-giving word of Jesus that John will turn in the following episode.

Return to Galilee. ⁴³When the two days were over, he left for Galilee. ⁴⁴(Jesus himself had testified that no one esteems a prophet in his own country.) ⁴⁵When he arrived in Galilee, the people there welcomed him. They themselves had been at the feast and had seen all that he had done in Jerusalem on that occasion. **Second Sign at Cana.** ⁴⁶He went to Cana in Galilee once more, where he had made the water wine. At Capernaum there happened to be a royal official whose son was ill. ⁴⁷When he heard that Jesus had come back from Judea to Galilee, he went to him and begged him to come down and restore health to his son, who was near death. ⁴⁸Jesus replied, "Unless you people see signs and wonders, you do not believe." ⁴⁹"Sir," the royal official pleaded with him, "come down before my child dies." ⁵⁰Jesus told him, "Return home. Your son will live." The man put his trust in the word Jesus spoke to him, and started for home.

⁵¹He was on his way there when his servants met him with the news that his boy was going to live. ⁵²When he asked them at what time the boy had shown

4:43-5:47 Episode II: Jesus' Life-Giving Word

This second thematic episode consists of three sections:
1. narrative healing of the official's son;
2. narrative healing of the infirm man at the pool;
3. discourse.
All three will emphasize the life-giving quality of Jesus' word.

1. Healing of the official's son (4:43-54). This account is prefaced by verses 43-45, which tie this incident to the preceding. Verse 44, ". . . no one esteems a prophet in his own country," is a bit strange. It is probably the author's way of saying that the people of Jesus' own Galilee were over-enchanted by miracles, and that the only proper response to Jesus at this point will be offered by a pagan official.

The story itself is strikingly similar to the Capernaum cure reported in both Matt 8:5-13 and Luke 7:1-10, but with the kinds of differences expected as the story was passed along in oral form. The sign-meaning of this "long-distance cure" is very clear. It is uniquely Jesus' word—he does nothing but speak—that gives life to this child "near death" (v. 47). *That* Jesus spoke is noted three times (vv. 50, 53); *what* he spoke is also mentioned three times (vv. 50, 51, 53). That is the insistence. Jesus' word gives life—to those who believe (vv. 50, 53).

The evangelist has couched Jesus' words in verse 48 in the plural: "Unless you (plural) people see signs and wonders, you (plural) do not believe." In so doing, he makes Jesus speak, not mainly to the quite admirable official, but to men and women of John's own day and ours. Thus, though the evangelist is willing to mention the signs (and this is now the second of them, says verse 54) and, perhaps, even to use an existing collection of them

23

improvement, they told him, "The fever left him yesterday afternoon about one." ⁵³It was at that very hour, the father realized, that Jesus had told him, "Your son is going to live." He and his whole household thereupon became believers. ⁵⁴This was the second sign that Jesus performed on returning from Judea to Galilee.

5 **Cure on a Sabbath Feast.** ¹Later, on the occasion of a Jewish feast, Jesus went up to Jerusalem. ²Now in Jerusalem by the Sheep Pool there is a place with the Hebrew name Bethesda. Its five porticoes ³were crowded with sick people lying there blind, lame or disabled [waiting for the movement of the water]. [⁴] ⁵There was one man who had been sick for thirty-eight years. ⁶Jesus, who knew he had been sick a long time, said

when he saw him lying there, "Do you want to be healed?" ⁷"Sir," the sick man answered, "I do not have anyone to plunge me into the pool once the water has been stirred up. By the time I get there, someone else has gone in ahead of me." ⁸Jesus said to him, "Stand up! Pick up your mat and walk!" ⁹The man was immediately cured; he picked up his mat and began to walk.

The day was a sabbath. ¹⁰Consequently, some of the Jews began telling the man who had been cured, "It is the sabbath, and you are not allowed to carry that mat around." ¹¹He explained: "It was the man who cured me who told me, 'Pick up your mat and walk.'" ¹²"This person who told you to pick it up and walk," they asked, "who is he?" ¹³The man who had been restored to

in his Gospel (2:11; 4:54; 20:30), he does not overestimate their efficacy. They are important if their deeper meaning is understood. What is more important is to stand open and receptive to the life-giving power of Jesus' word.

2. Healing of the infirm man at the pool (5:1-18). This incident takes place in Jerusalem at a Jewish feast that John does not identify. What is important for him, and for us, is that it occurs on a sabbath (vv. 9-10, 16, 18). The pool has been located by modern archaeologists next to the Crusader Church of St. Anne. The excavations have shown that the pool was enclosed rectangularly by four porticoes, with a fifth running across the pool and dividing it into two sections. (John's knowledge of Jerusalem is good.)

Our text lacks a fourth verse, which speaks of an angel descending to move the water. This verse is missing in our oldest and best Greek manuscripts dating back to the second and fourth centuries, and was probably added by someone who wished to attribute the moving of the water in verse 7 to a direct heavenly intervention. The original text says simply that the water bubbled up on occasion and that healing power was attributed to it.

This sign-miracle follows the preceding one in rapid succession because it has the same theological bi-level, and John wants the two together to reinforce his teaching at this point. Again, it is Jesus' word—and only that— which gives life to a man whose body has been devitalized for thirty-eight years. And again, *what* Jesus spoke, "Pick up your mat and walk," is mentioned in almost identical terms three times (vv. 8, 11, 12).

health had no idea who it was. The crowd in that place was so great that Jesus had been able to slip away.

¹⁴Later on, Jesus found him in the temple precincts and said to him: "Remember, now, you have been cured. Give up your sins so that something worse may not overtake you." ¹⁵The man went off and informed the Jews that Jesus was the one who had cured him.

Discourse on His Sabbath Work. ¹⁶It was because Jesus did things such as this on the sabbath that they began to persecute him. ¹⁷But he had an answer for them:

"My Father is at work until now, and I am at work as well."

¹⁸The reason why the Jews were even more determined to kill him was that he not only was breaking the sabbath but, worse still, was speaking of God as his own Father, thereby making himself God's equal.

The Work of the Son

¹⁹This was Jesus' answer:

"I solemnly assure you,
the Son cannot do anything by himself—
he can do only what he sees the Father doing.
For whatever the Father does,
the Son does likewise.
20 For the Father loves the Son
and everything the Father does he shows him.
Yes, to your great wonderment,
he will show him even greater works than these.

One instructive yet sad part of the story is that the cured man, though he has directly seen and benefited from the sign, has not understood it. To him the sign has not revealed its meaning. He heads off to inform the adversaries that it was Jesus who had healed him and for whom they were looking (v. 15).

Verses 16-18 lead us from the narrative into the discourse, in which the theological meaning of the two cures will be spelled out in full. The early mention of the sabbath (v. 9) becomes important. To carry around a sleeping mat on the sabbath was contrary to the law. Yet Jesus authorized the action. In initial response to his critics (v. 17), Jesus compares himself to his Father. Since the Father works on the sabbath, as on all days, so can Jesus. This response is dangerous, since it places Jesus and the Father on a similar (equal?) plane. And so the dramatic plot thickens. Who is this Jesus who treats both God and the sabbath as his own family possessions?

Here again we are caught up, I believe, in a historical bi-level. The questions arising in verses 16-18 (sabbath rest and Jesus' divinity) are precisely those that John's own community faced in its dialogue with the Jews of its own neighborhood. Was Jesus really divine? What did the sabbath mean and enjoin for Christian Jews? The following discourse will treat the specific question of Jesus' relationship to his Father at greater depth.

3. The discourse (5:19-47). The main reason for considering units 1–3, the two cures and this discourse, as one literary unit is that all sections sound the one theme: the life-giving power of Jesus' word. He has just healed the official's son by saying, "Return home. Your son will live" (4:50),

21 Indeed, just as the Father raises the dead and grants life, so the Son grants life to those to whom he wishes.

22 The Father himself judges no one, but has assigned all judgment to the Son,

23 so that all men may honor the Son just as they honor the Father. He who refuses to honor the Son refuses to honor the Father who sent him.

24 I solemnly assure you, the man who hears my word and has faith in him who sent me possesses eternal life. He does not come under condemnation, but has passed from death to life.

25 I solemnly assure you, an hour is coming, has indeed come, when the dead shall hear the voice of the Son of God, and those who have heeded it shall live.

and the infirm man with the words, "Pick up your mat and walk" (5:8). And now the discourse will underscore the theological depth of this same truth. Note how the words of Jesus keep coming back to this teaching:

"Indeed, just as the Father raises the dead and grants life, so the *Son grants life* to those to whom he wishes" (v. 21).

"I solemnly assure you, the man who *hears my word* and has faith in him who sent me *possesses eternal life*. . . . *He has passed from death to life*" (v. 24).

"I solemnly assure you, an hour is coming, has indeed come, when the dead shall *hear the voice of the Son of God*, and those who have heeded it *shall live*. Indeed, just as the Father possesses life in himself, so has he granted it to the Son to have life in himself" (vv. 25-26).

". . . for an hour is coming in which all those in their tombs [like Lazarus in chapter 11] *shall hear his voice and come forth*" (v. 28).

What has happened in John's construction is that Jesus' right to work on the sabbath because his Father works has developed into a consideration of the relationship between Father and Son on a more elevated and more general level. Notwithstanding the Jewish commandment of sabbath rest, it was always recognized that God's two primary activities did not, and could not, cease on the sabbath: these were the divine acts of life-giving and of judgment. Both formed a constant part of God's life: babies were born and people did die on the sabbath. Our present discourse insists that what God does, the Son also does. The Father gives life, and so too does the Son, by his word. And a new point enters into consideration. As the Father judges, so too does the Son (vv. 22, 27, 30). In the Fourth Gospel, however, this judgment is not projected for the future. It occurs right now, depending on one's attitude toward Jesus. Whoever hears and accepts him receives eternal life and does not come under judgment (v. 24), since he or she thus hears and accepts the Father. Whoever responds negatively judges himself or herself by that very fact.

26 Indeed, just as the Father possesses life in himself,
so has he granted it to the Son to have life in himself.

27 The Father has given over to him power to pass judgment because he is Son of Man;

28 no need for you to be surprised at this,
for an hour is coming in which all those in their tombs shall hear his voice and come forth.

29 Those who have done right shall rise to live;
the evildoers shall rise to be damned.

30 I cannot do anything of myself.
I judge as I hear,
and my judgment is honest because I am not seeking my own will
but the will of him who sent me.

Witnesses to Jesus

31 "If I witness on my own behalf,
you cannot verify my testimony;

32 but there is another who is testifying on my behalf,
and the testimony he renders me I know can be verified.

33 You have sent to John,
who has testified to the truth.

34 (Not that I myself accept such human testimony—
I refer to these things only for your salvation.)

35 He was the lamp, set aflame and burning bright,
and for a while you exulted willingly in his light.

36 Yet I have testimony greater than John's,
namely, the works the Father has given me to accomplish.
These very works which I perform

Now all of this—and one can justly imagine our author arguing the various points with his neighboring non-Christian Jews—leads to the impossible, incredible question: If this is all true, is not Jesus God, which, since the Father is certainly God, makes for two Gods? The language of the discourse becomes very circumspect at this point. Our author is certain of two facts—the divinity of Jesus and the oneness of God—which neither he nor the whole of Christian tradition has been able to reconcile completely, though believing in them ardently. The best John can do is to insist on the divinity of Jesus, while insisting equally on his dependence and obedience. And so here, as elsewhere when Jesus' divinity is stated, the discourse is also intent upon noting that "the Son cannot do anything by himself" (v. 19); that "everything the Father does he shows" the Son (v. 20); that the Father "has assigned all judgment to the Son" (v. 22); that the Father "has granted it to the Son to have life" and "has given over to him power to pass judgment" (vv. 26-27). In a word, and a strong word it is, "I cannot do anything of myself" (v. 30). Our author's predicament is clear, and we too are involved in it. Jesus, divine as he is, is not the Father; and the Father is God. Little wonder that Jewish Christians of the first century had difficulty explaining Jesus to their fellow Jews.

The final section of the discourse details the various witnesses that testify to Jesus. Above all, there is the Father himself who renders testimony (vv. 31-32). And there is John the Baptist for those who have been im-

testify on my behalf
that the Father has sent me.

37 Moreover, the Father who sent me
has himself given testimony on my
behalf.
His voice you have never heard,
his form you have never seen,

38 neither do you have his word abiding in your hearts
because you do not believe
the One he has sent.

39 Search the Scriptures
in which you think you have eternal
life—
they also testify on my behalf.

40 Yet you are unwilling to come to me
to possess that life.

Unbelief of Jesus' Hearers

41 "It is not that I accept human
praise—

42 it is simply that I know you,

and you do not have the love of
God in your hearts.

43 I have come in my Father's name,
yet you do not accept me.
But let someone come in his own
name
and him you will accept.

44 How can people like you believe,
when you accept praise from one
another
yet do not seek the glory that comes
from the One [God]?

45 Do not imagine that I will be your
accuser before the Father;
the one to accuse you is Moses
on whom you have set your hopes.

46 If you believed Moses
you would then believe me,
for it was about me that he wrote.

47 But if you do not believe what he
wrote,
how can you believe what I say?"

pressed by him (vv. 33-36). Then there are the works that Jesus has done
through his Father's power, works that are visible words revealing both
Father and Son (vv. 36-37). Finally—and this argument is aimed peculiarly
at the Jewish community—there are the words of Scripture and Moses
himself that testify to Jesus (vv. 39-47). "If you believed Moses you would
then believe me, for it was about me that he wrote" (v. 46). In the episode
that follows, we shall see an example of how this Old Testament scripture
could be utilized to evolve and describe a further theological characteristic
of Jesus: his power to nourish as the bread of life.

6:1-71 Episode III: Jesus as the Bread of Life

This chapter will center on the one theme of Jesus as the bread of life. It
has four clear divisions: (1) the multiplication of the loaves; (2) walking on
the water; (3) the discourse; and (4) an epilogue of reactions.

Before speaking at all of the loaves miracle, it might be well to notice
what has often been presented as a real difficulty in the order of John's
Gospel and a possible proof that somehow, in its earliest history, its pages
got mixed up. At the end of chapter 4, Jesus is found in Galilee. In 5:1 he
goes up to Jerusalem. But in 6:1 he is again in Galilee. Geographically this is
strange, to say the least, so that some commentators have suggested that
chapter 6 be placed before chapter 5. None of the Greek manuscripts has

6 **Multiplication of the Loaves at Passover.** [1]Later on, Jesus crossed the Sea of Galilee [to the shore] of Tiberias; [2]a vast crowd kept following him because they saw the signs he was performing for the sick. [3]Jesus then went up the mountain and sat down there with his disciples. [4]The Jewish feast of Passover was near; [5]when Jesus looked up and caught sight of a vast crowd coming toward him, he said to Philip, "Where shall we buy bread for these people to eat?" [6](He knew well what he intended to do but he asked this to test Philip's response.) [7]Philip replied, "Not even with two hundred days' wages could we buy loaves enough to give each of them a mouthful!"

[8]One of Jesus' disciples, Andrew, Simon Peter's brother, remarked to him, [9]"There is a lad here who has five barley loaves and a couple of dried fish, but what good is that for so many?" [10]Jesus said, "Get the people to recline." Even though the men numbered about five thousand, there was plenty of grass for them to find a place on the ground. [11]Jesus then took the loaves of bread, gave thanks, and passed them around to those reclining there; he did the same with the dried fish, as much as they wanted. [12]When they had had enough, he told his disciples, "Gather up the crusts that are left over so that nothing will go to waste." [13]At this, they gathered twelve baskets full of pieces left

this suggested reordering, and there are many good reasons for keeping the present disposition, while realizing that John need not be nearly so much interested in historical-geographical order as in organizing themes. Chapter 6, I believe, belongs where it is as a demonstration of the statement in 5:46-47 that Moses and Scripture refer to Jesus. This, as we shall see, is precisely what the discourse in chapter 6 will expound. I believe, too, that the reference to the sick in 6:2 points *back* to the identical Greek phrasing in 5:3. Finally, leaving chapters 5 and 6 in their present order gives us a combination of word and bread, the essential elements and order of Christian Eucharist, a combination that need not have escaped John's attention.

1. The multiplication of the loaves (6:1-15). The Jewish Passover (v. 4) was an unleavened bread feast, so the reference prepares us for the bread miracle that is about to take place. *This miracle is the only one narrated by all four evangelists:* by Mark twice, in 6:31-44 and 8:1-10; by Matthew twice, in 14:13-21 and 15:32-38; by Luke in 9:10-17. It must be that the primitive Christian Eucharist made the prefiguring loaves miracle common property in all the Christian communities. And, indeed, what Jesus does with the bread sounds like the rubrics for what the Christian minister continually did in the celebration of the Eucharist. In the accounts of Mark, Matthew, and Luke, Jesus *took* the bread and *blessed* and *broke* and *gave*. So would the Christian minister. John's description is equally ceremonial, but with one even more Christian peculiarity. In 6:11, Jesus took, *gave thanks*, and gave. The Greek for "give thanks" is *eucharisteō*, which gives us our word for Christian Eucharist. It occurs again in 6:23. This same Eucharistic overtone is heard again in verses 12-13, where the fish have disap-

over by those who had been fed with the five barley loaves.

14When the people saw the sign he had performed they began to say, "This is undoubtedly the Prophet who is to come into the world." 15At that, Jesus realized that they would come and carry him off to make him king, so he fled back to the mountain alone.

Walking on the Sea. 16As evening drew on, his disciples came down to the lake. 17They embarked, intending to cross the lake toward Capernaum. By this time it was dark, and Jesus had still not joined them; 18moreover, with a strong wind blowing, the sea was becoming rough. 19Finally, when they had rowed three or four miles, they

peared from the discussion, which speaks exclusively of the bread and the care to be taken of the remaining fragments. The ultimate *sign* (v. 14) of this miracle points to Jesus as the bread of life, particularly in the Eucharist.

The reaction in verse 14, "This is undoubtedly the Prophet who is to come into the world," refers again (as in 1:21, 24) to the prophet like Moses (Deut 18:15, 18) who was expected in the final days. Jesus has just fed the people with bread; Moses did the same with the desert manna.

One final note of interest is that the two disciples who function in this manifestation of Jesus to the crowd are Philip and Andrew, the same two who in 1:41, 45 acted as apostles to Nathaniel and Simon Peter, and who will later be apostles to the Greeks (12:20-22). Their role in the Fourth Gospel is to reach out.

2. Walking on the water (6:16-24). It is striking that John's sequence — the loaves miracle followed by that on the Sea of Galilee — is identical to that of Mark 6:34-51 and Matthew 14:13-33. The tradition of this ordering must be very old. In all three accounts Jesus calms his disciples with the identical majestic phrase: "It is I; do not be afraid" (John 6:20; Mark 6:50; Matt 14:27). As we shall see later, this phrasing, which in the Greek has no predicate and simply reads *egō eimi = I am*, has strong overtones of divinity, echoing the name for Yahweh found in Isa 43:10, 13, 25. Jesus is the divine presence; the disciples need have no fear.

There is a question as to why the water miracle should be situated at this point in a chapter that otherwise speaks exclusively of bread. What is it a sign of? No answer is completely satisfactory, but the following have been offered. (a) The Old Testament Passover miracles were manna bread plus the crossing of the Reed Sea, and water springing from the rock. Exod 14-16 ties together in tight sequence the account of the Reed Sea crossing and the gift of the desert manna. This traditional Exodus coupling of water and bread, found also in Ps 78:13-25, may have encouraged the first Jewish Christians to attach the Christian water-sign to that of the bread. They are so found in Mark 6, Matt 14, and now in John 6. (b) John is simply extending his theme of life-giving word by presenting Jesus as life-giver in time of famine and of storm. (c) The storm scene is intended as a sign of Jesus'

sighted Jesus approaching the boat, walking on the water. They were frightened, [20]but he told them, "It is I; do not be afraid." [21]They wanted to take him into the boat, but suddenly it came aground on the shore they had been approaching. [22]The crowd remained on the other side of the lake. The next day they realized that there had been only one boat there and that Jesus had not left in it with his disciples; rather, they had set out by themselves. [23]Then some boats came out from Tiberias near the place where they had eaten the bread after the Lord had given thanks. [24]Once the crowd saw that neither Jesus nor his disciples were there, they too embarked in the boats and went to Capernaum looking for Jesus.

Discourse on the Bread of Life. [25]When they found him on the other side of the lake, they said to him, "Rabbi, when did you come here?" [26]Jesus answered them:

"I assure you,
you are not looking for me because you have seen signs
but because you have eaten your fill of the loaves.
[27] You should not be working for perishable food

divine status (the "It is I" of verse 19 masks the profound I AM of the original Greek) and his ever-helping presence, "do not be afraid" (v. 20).

The account closes (vv. 21-24) with the boat suddenly coming to land (this is seemingly miraculous too) and the crowd, or part of it, transferring itself to Capernaum to find Jesus. This will provide the audience for the discourse that now follows.

3. The discourse (6:26-59). The best way to understand this discourse is to recognize that it is a homily based on Jesus' teaching but elaborated extensively by a Christian preacher aided by Jesus' Spirit. In this sense, the whole discourse comes from the Lord. It centers on one biblical text, "He gave them bread from the heavens to eat" (v. 31), and is therefore a conscious demonstration of the truth of 5:39, 46-47 that the Scriptures elucidate the person of Jesus. The pivotal text is a loose, by-memory combination of several possible Old Testament quotations:

Exod 16:4: "I will now rain down *bread from heaven* for you";

Neh 9:15: "*Food from heaven you gave* them in their hunger";

Ps 78:24: "He rained manna upon them for food and *gave* them *heavenly bread*";

Ps 105:40: ". . . and with *bread from heaven* he satisfied them."

All or some of these associated texts have been combined by the preacher into the one amalgam of verse 31. The homily is broken by the short interruptions of verses 30-31, 34, 41-43, 52, which, by introducing live dialogue, help to keep the audience's interest while at the same time pointing out the precise difficulties felt by both the Jews of Jesus' time and of John's own later period.

but for food that remains unto life
eternal,
food which the Son of Man will
give you;
it is on him that God the Father has
set his seal."

²⁸At this they said to him, "What must
we do to perform the works of God?"
²⁹Jesus replied:

"This is the work of God:
have faith in the One whom he
sent."

³⁰"So that we can put faith in you," they
asked him, "what sign are you going to
perform for us to see? What is the 'work'
you do? ³¹Our ancestors had manna to
eat in the desert; according to Scripture,
'He gave them bread from the heavens to
eat.'" ³²Jesus said to them:

"I solemnly assure you,
it was not Moses who gave you
bread from the heavens;
it is my Father who gives you the
real heavenly bread.
³³ God's bread comes down from
heaven
and gives life to the world."

³⁴"Sir, give us this bread always," they
besought him.

³⁵Jesus explained to them:

"I myself am the bread of life.

No one who comes to me shall ever
be hungry,
no one who believes in me shall
ever thirst.
³⁶ But as I told you—
though you have seen me, you still
do not believe.
³⁷ All that the Father gives me shall
come to me;
no one who comes will I ever reject,
³⁸ because it is not to do my own will
that I have come down from
heaven,
but to do the will of him who sent
me.
³⁹ It is the will of him who sent me
that I should lose nothing of what
he has given me;
rather, that I should raise it up on
the last day.
⁴⁰ Indeed, this is the will of my Father,
that everyone who looks upon the
Son
and believes in him
shall have eternal life.
Him I will raise up on the last day."

⁴¹At this the Jews started to murmur in
protest because he claimed, "I am the
bread that came down from heaven."
⁴²They kept saying: "Is this not Jesus, the
son of Joseph? Do we not know his
father and mother? How can he claim to
have come down from heaven?"

This homily on a biblical text—what the Jews would call a *midrash*—
follows a phrase-by-phrase order. It will treat in order: *He gave; bread from
heaven; to eat.* Let's observe this happen.

a) *He gave* (vv. 26-34). In this first section, the emphasis lies on the giving. Jesus will give (vv. 27, 34), not as Moses gave (v. 32) a perishable
manna food of mortality, but as the Father, source of eternal life, gives (v.
32). Thus far, Jesus appears as the giver of bread and therefore as the new
and superior Moses.

b) *Bread from heaven* (vv. 35-47). The insistence now shifts to the bread
from heaven that Jesus not only gives but actually is (vv. 35, 38, 41, 42). It
is important to note here that the operative verb is "believe." Jesus as bread
from heaven is accepted and consumed through the belief required in verses

⁴³"Stop your murmuring," Jesus told them.

⁴⁴ "No one can come to me
unless the Father who sent me draws him;
I will raise him up on the last day.
⁴⁵ It is written in the prophets:
'They shall all be taught by God.'
Everyone who has heard the Father
and learned from him
comes to me.
⁴⁶ Not that anyone has seen the Father—
only the one who is from God
has seen the Father.
⁴⁷ Let me firmly assure you,
he who believes has eternal life.
⁴⁸ I am the bread of life.
⁴⁹ Your ancestors ate manna in the desert, but they died.
⁵⁰ This is the bread that comes down from heaven
for a man to eat and never die.
⁵¹ I myself am the living bread
come down from heaven.
If anyone eats this bread
he shall live forever;
the bread I will give

is my flesh, for the life of the world."

⁵²At this the Jews quarreled among themselves, saying, "How can he give us his flesh to eat?" ⁵³Thereupon Jesus said to them:
"Let me solemnly assure you,
if you do not eat the flesh of the Son of Man
and drink his blood,
you have no life in you.
⁵⁴ He who feeds on my flesh
and drinks my blood
has life eternal,
and I will raise him up on the last day.
⁵⁵ For my flesh is real food
and my blood real drink.
⁵⁶ The man who feeds on my flesh
and drinks my blood
remains in me, and I in him.
⁵⁷ Just as the Father who has life sent me
and I have life because of the Father,
so the man who feeds on me
will have life because of me.
⁵⁸ This is the bread that came down

35, 36, 40, 47. What this means is that this is a faith nourishment. Jesus is bread from heaven, feeding all believers, in the same sense that Old Testament wisdom nourished all who accepted it (Prov 9:1-5). We might call this type of feeding "sapiential."

c) *To eat* (vv. 48-59). In this final section, the vocabulary changes radically. The significant words are "flesh," "blood," "*eat*," "drink." Note the constant repetition of "eat" and "feed on" (an even more physical verb in the Greek than "eat") in verses 49, 50, 51, 52, 53, 54, 57, 58. These verbs become overwhelmingly insistent, as does the constant reference to flesh and blood, food and drink. The meaning of the discourse has changed. Where in the preceding section Jesus nourished through wisdom-revelation those who believed, the verb "believe" has now completely disappeared and is replaced by "eat," "feed on." Our homilist is clearly speaking now of *sacramental* nourishment, of the food and drink that one eats and feeds upon, of the Eucharistic nourishment provided by the flesh and blood of the Son of Man (v. 53). The "Son of Man" phraseology tells us that this is not the physical

from heaven.
Unlike your ancestors who ate and
died nonetheless,
the man who feeds on this bread
shall live forever."

⁵⁹He said this in a synagogue instruction at Capernaum.

Effect of the Discourse. ⁶⁰After hearing his words, many of his disciples remarked, "This sort of talk is hard to endure! How can anyone take it seriously?" ⁶¹Jesus was fully aware that his disciples were murmuring in protest at what he had said. "Does it shake your faith?" he asked them.

62 "What, then, if you were to see the
Son of Man
ascend to where he was
before . . .?
63 It is the spirit that gives life;

flesh and blood of the earthly Jesus that we are asked to eat and drink but the spiritual, Spirit-filled flesh and blood of the heavenly Son of Man. Verse 58 ties the homily together by referring back to the central phrase of verse 31.

What this homily has done, therefore, is to deliver a rich and multi-faceted exposition of the Jesus-as-Bread-of-Life theme. Jesus is first of all the *giver* of the bread, a new Moses. He is also the *bread of wisdom and revelation* who nourishes all who come to him in faith. He is, finally, the *Eucharistic* source of eternal life for all who eat and drink the flesh and blood of the heavenly and glorified Son of Man. Because John uses this Eucharistic material in this Bread of Life homily, it will not be too surprising —yet surprising enough—that the Eucharist will not be mentioned at the Last Supper. Its material has been transferred to this incident. John has also succeeded, with this transfer, to unite in this one chapter the essentials of Christian Eucharist, the word and the bread—the revealing word of verses 35-47 and the sacramental bread of verses 48-59.

4. Epilogue of various reactions (6:60-71). These final verses resume the murmuring criticisms of verses 41-43, 52 to describe a mounting crisis of faith for Jesus' disciples: "This sort of talk is hard to endure! How can anyone take it seriously?" (v. 60). At this point in the text, our historical bi-levels (Jesus' time and John's later period) reappear. If these verses refer to Jesus' Galilean ministry, in which he hardly would have spoken of the Last Supper Eucharist, the critical reactions refer solely to the material of verses 26-47, and are a negative response to his presentation of himself as object of faith, as bread-wisdom giving life to those who believe in him. But the passage as a whole certainly reflects also the crisis (present for all Christian centuries) of John's own community, the difficulty involved in accepting Jesus as the sacramental bread of life. To this difficulty will be added the scandal of the ascent of the Son of Man "to where he was before" (v. 62). The first step of that ascent will be Jesus' elevation onto a cross on top of a hill.

the flesh is useless.
The words I spoke to you
are spirit and life.
⁶⁴ Yet among you there are some who
do not believe."

(Jesus knew from the start, of course, the ones who refused to believe, and the one who would hand him over.)
⁶⁵He went on to say:

"This is why I have told you
that no one can come to me
unless it is granted him by the
Father."

⁶⁶From this time on, many of his disciples broke away and would not remain in his company any longer. ⁶⁷Jesus then said to the Twelve, "Do you want to leave me too?" ⁶⁸Simon Peter answered him, "Lord, to whom shall we go? You have the words of eternal life. ⁶⁹We have come to believe; we are convinced that you are God's holy one." ⁷⁰Jesus replied, "Did I not choose the Twelve of you myself? Yet one of you is a devil." ⁷¹(He was talking about Judas, son of Simon the Iscariot, who, though one of the Twelve, was going to hand Jesus over.)

7 **Feast of Booths.** ¹After this, Jesus moved about within Galilee. He had decided not to travel in Judea because some of the Jews were looking for a chance to kill him. ²However, as the Jewish feast of Booths drew near, ³his brothers had this to say: "You ought to

The chapter concludes (vv. 66-71) with a presentation of two models. Peter is one. He takes the risk, opening himself to the Word whose revealing words give eternal life. "Lord, to whom shall we go? You have the words of eternal life. We have come to believe; we are convinced that you are God's holy one" (vv. 68-69). The other model is Judas. He will remain in the group, living a divided existence, but already moving into darkness and into the demonic power which that darkness symbolizes (13:26-30). His appearance here as future betrayer (v. 71) lends further proof to the belief that John is using Last Supper material in this latter part of the discourse to complete his total presentation of Jesus as the bread of life for the Christian community.

One final observation before leaving this rich chapter: verses 67, 70-71 speak of "the Twelve." Only here and in 20:24 (Thomas) does John use this terminology. He speaks, rather, and so very often, of "the disciples," his favorite description of Jesus' followers. John leans much more toward the equality of discipleship than the grading of hierarchy.

7:1–8:59 Episode IV: Identity Crisis

These two chapters, in which Jesus is both manifested and rejected as the prophet, Christ, the unique Son of the Father, and the divine I AM (*egō eimi*) are among the most difficult to synthesize in the Gospel. There is such an overwhelming richness of movement and content that the chapters are strongly resistant to external ordering by a commentator. Yet, elements of structural and theological order can be found.

leave here and go to Judea so that your disciples there may see the works you are performing. ⁴No one who wishes to be known publicly keeps his actions hidden. If you are going to do things like these, you may as well display yourself to the world at large." ⁵(As a matter of fact, not even his brothers had much confidence in him.) ⁶Jesus answered them:

"It is not yet the right time for me, whereas the time is always right for you.
⁷ The world is incapable of hating you,
but it does hate me
because of the evidence I bring against it
that what it does is evil.
⁸Go up yourselves to the festival. I am not going up to this festival because the time is not yet ripe for me." ⁹Having said this, he stayed on in Galilee. ¹⁰However, once his brothers had gone up to the festival he too went up, but as if in secret and not for all to see.

¹¹During the festival, naturally, the Jews were looking for him, asking, "Where is that troublemaker?" ¹²Among the crowds there was much guarded

1. Introduction (7:1-14). (a) The background of these chapters is the Jewish feast of Booths (or Tents or Tabernacles) — *Sukkoth* in Hebrew — an annual autumn feast of thanksgiving for the yearly harvest and for the historic Exodus miracles of the water and pillar of fire. The feast, similar to our Thanksgiving, was the most joyous and popular of the Jewish calendar; and during it the celebrants lived in branched huts reminiscent of those used during the harvest time and the desert wandering.

Two distinctive features of this week-long ceremony in September–October have made an impression on the text. Water was brought daily from the pool of Siloam to the temple, where it was poured over the altar as prayers were recited for the all-important winter rain. And the lights in the women's court flamed so brightly that the city was lit up by them. Water and light play a fairly important part in these two chapters.

b) The brothers (7:3-10) fare poorly in this episode. They see and cannot deny the works that Jesus is doing; yet their suggestion that Jesus should go public in Jerusalem, the heart and capital of the country, is banal and incorrect. Verse 5 reads literally: "neither did his brothers believe in him." This agrees with the picture of Jesus' family given in Mark 3:21, 31-35; 6:4. Happily, the brothers do form part of the post-resurrection church in Acts 1:14. They, too, had to struggle through failure into the Christian faith.

c) In general, chapters 7 and 8 report a hectic clash of dialogues and controversies as the Gospel turns toward the passion. Deep within the rapid disagreements lie the theological disputes that brought Jesus to the cross and, years later, forced John's community out of the synagogue.

d) The two chapters are linked together by their content, which repeats again and again the issues under discussion, and also by what is commonly called "literary inclusion," a statement toward the beginning that will be

debate about him. Some maintained, "He is a good man," while others kept saying, "Not at all—he is only misleading the crowd!" ¹³No one dared talk openly about him, however, for fear of the Jews. **First Episode.** ¹⁴The feast was half over by the time Jesus went into the temple area and began to teach. ¹⁵The Jews were filled with amazement and said, "How did this man get his education when he had no teacher?" ¹⁶This was Jesus' answer:

"My doctrine is not my own;
it comes from him who sent me.
¹⁷ Any man who chooses to do his will
will know about this doctrine—
namely, whether it comes from God
or is simply spoken on my own.
¹⁸ Whoever speaks on his own
is bent on self-glorification.
The man who seeks glory for him
who sent him is truthful;
there is no dishonesty in his heart.

¹⁹ Moses has given you the law, has he not?
Yet not one of you keeps it.
Why do you look for a chance to kill me?"

²⁰"You are mad!" the crowd retorted. "Who wants to kill you?" ²¹Jesus answered:

"I have performed a single work
and you profess astonishment over it.
²² Moses gave you circumcision
(though it did not originate with Moses but with the patriarchs).
And so, even on a sabbath you circumcise a man.
²³ If a man can be circumcised on the sabbath
to prevent a violation of Mosaic law,
how is it you are angry with me
for curing a whole man on the sabbath?

balanced, like two bookends, by a similar expression at the end. In this instance, the "hidden" (v. 4) and "in secret" (v. 10)—both *en kryptō* in the original Greek text—are counterbalanced by the use of the same Greek root *ekrybē*, "hid himself," in 8:59. These bookends show that the author intends that these two chapters form a unit.

2. Parallel structure of 7:14-53. It is clear that this long section has been arranged into direct parallels, with the initial division of 7:14-36 neatly balanced by its equivalent in 7:37-52. At issue are the initial questions as to whether Jesus is the Christ and the prophet of Deut 18:15, 18.

a) *Jesus' teaching* (7:14-24). His doctrine is not his own but comes from God who sent him. Jesus speaks this doctrine faithfully. They, on the contrary, do not keep the law of Moses, which they profess. Why is it that they can circumcise on the sabbath but become so irate when Jesus cures a man on the sabbath? (5:1-10).

a') *Jesus' teaching* (7:37-39). On the last day of the week-long feast, Jesus invites all who thirst to come to him. Either from Jesus himself (the Greek text here is uncertain) or from those who believe in him will flow the rivers of living water, the Spirit. But the Spirit has not yet been given, nor will be given, until Jesus is glorified through the cross and resurrection.

24 Stop judging by appearances
   and make an honest judgment."

25This led some of the people of Jerusalem to remark: "Is this not the one they want to kill? 26Here he is speaking in public and they don't say a word to him! Perhaps even the authorities have decided that this is the Messiah. 27Still, we know where this man is from. When the Messiah comes, no one is supposed to know his origins."

28At this, Jesus, who was teaching in the temple area, cried out:

"So you know me,
   and you know my origins?
The truth is, I have not come of
   myself.
I was sent by One who has the right
   to send,
and him you do not know.
29 I know him
   because it is from him I come:
   he sent me."

30At this they tried to seize him, but no one laid a finger on him because his hour had not yet come. 31Many in the crowd came to believe in him. They kept saying, "When the Messiah comes, can he be expected to perform more signs than this man?" 32The Pharisees overheard this debate about him among the crowd, and the chief priests and Pharisees together sent temple guard to arrest him. 33Jesus then said to them:

"Only a little while longer am I to be
   with you,
then I am going away to him who
   sent me.
34 You will look for me, but you will
   not find me;
where I am you cannot come."

35This caused the Jews to exclaim among themselves: "Where does he intend to go that we will not find him? Surely he is not going off to the Diaspora among the Greeks, to teach them? 36What does he mean by saying, 'You will look for me, but you will not find me,' and, 'Where I am you cannot come'?"

Second Episode. 37On the last and greatest day of the festival, Jesus stood up and cried out:

"If anyone thirsts, let him come to
   me;
let him drink 38who believes in me.
Scripture has it:
'From within him rivers of living
   water shall flow.'"

39(Here he was referring to the Spirit, whom those that came to believe in him were to receive. There was, of course, no Spirit as yet, since Jesus had not yet been glorified.)

40Some in the crowd who heard these words began to say, "This must be the Prophet." 41Others were claiming, "He is the Messiah." But an objection was raised: "Surely the Messiah is not to

---

b) *Discussion about Jesus* (7:25-31). The question here is whether or not Jesus is the Christ (vv. 26-27, 31).

b') *Discussion about Jesus* (7:40-44). The discussion continues as to whether Jesus is the Christ (vv. 41-42) and expands to ask whether he is the prophet of Deut 18:15, 18. (John's admittance that the Christ should be born in Bethlehem [v. 42] is strong proof that he himself believed that Jesus was born there.)

come from Galilee? ⁴²Does not Scripture say that the Messiah, being of David's family, is to come from Bethlehem, the village where David lived?" ⁴³In this fashion the crowd was sharply divided over him. ⁴⁴Some of them even wanted to apprehend him. However, no one laid hands on him.

⁴⁵When the temple guards came back, the chief priests and Pharisees asked them, "Why did you not bring him in?" ⁴⁶"No man ever spoke like that before," the guards replied. ⁴⁷"Do not tell us you too have been taken in!" the Pharisees retorted. ⁴⁸"You do not see any of the Sanhedrin believing in him, do you? Or the Pharisees? ⁴⁹Only this lot, that knows nothing about the law—and they are lost anyway!" ⁵⁰One of their own number, Nicodemus (the man who had come to him), spoke up to say, ⁵¹"Since when does our law condemn any man without first hearing him and knowing the facts?" ⁵²"Do not tell us you are a Galilean too," they taunted him. "Look it up. You will not find the Prophet coming from Galilee."

8 **The Adulteress.** [⁵³Then each went off to his own house, ¹while Jesus went out to the Mount of Olives. ²At daybreak he reappeared in the temple area; and when the people started com-

ing to him, he sat down and began to teach them. ³The scribes and the Pharisees led a woman forward who had been caught in adultery. They made her stand there in front of everyone. ⁴"Teacher," they said to him, "this woman has been caught in the act of adultery. ⁵In the law, Moses ordered such women to be stoned. What do you have to say about the case?" ⁶(They were posing this question to trap him, so that they could have something to accuse him of.) Jesus bent down and started tracing on the ground with his finger. ⁷When they persisted in their questioning, he straightened up and said to them, "Let the man among you who has no sin be the first to cast a stone at her." ⁸A second time he bent down and wrote on the ground. ⁹Then the audience drifted away one by one, beginning with the elders. This left him alone with the woman, who continued to stand there before him. ¹⁰Jesus finally straightened up and said to her, "Woman, where did they all disappear to? Has no one condemned you?" ¹¹"No one, sir," she answered. Jesus said, "Nor do I condemn you. You may go. But from now on, avoid this sin."]

Third Episode. ¹²Jesus spoke to them once again:

---

c) *Temple officers* (7:32-36) are sent by the chief priests and Pharisees to arrest Jesus. He responds that he will be with them for just a little while. Will he go to the Diaspora (v. 35), to the lands outside of Palestine to which, in fact, Christianity spread after Jesus' death?

c') *Temple officers* (7:45-52) report back to the priests and Pharisees that Jesus speaks as did no one previously, but their report is treated with authoritarian scorn. Nicodemus, passing from the night of 3:2 into considerably more light, defends Jesus, but to no avail.

3. Intense disputes (8:12-59). The clear and simple paralleling in the previous chapter disappears with our present material, in which there is a steady alternating of statements and responses on the part of Jesus and his opponents—the chief priests and Pharisees from verses 13-19, and the Jews

"I am the light of the world.
No follower of mine shall ever walk
    in darkness;
no, he shall possess the light of life."

13This caused the Pharisees to break in
with: "You are your own witness. Such
testimony cannot be valid." 14Jesus
answered:

"What if I am my own witness?
My testimony is valid nonetheless,
because I know where I came from
and where I am going;
you know neither the one nor the
    other.
15 You pass judgment according to ap-
    pearances
but I pass judgment on no man.
16 Even if I do judge,
that judgment of mine is valid
because I am not alone:
I have at my side the One who sent
    me [the Father].
17 It is laid down in your law
that evidence given by two persons
    is valid.
18 I am one of those testifying in my
    behalf,
the Father who sent me is the
    other."

19They pressed him: "And where is this
'Father' of yours?" Jesus replied:

"You know neither me nor my
    Father.
If you knew me, you would know
my Father too."

20He spoke these words while teaching at
the temple treasury. Still, he went un-
apprehended, because his hour had not
yet come.

Warning to Unbelievers. 21Again he
said to them:

"I am going away. You will look
    for me
but you will die in your sins.
Where I am going you cannot
    come."

22At this some of the Jews began to ask,
"Does he mean he will kill himself when
he claims, 'Where I am going you cannot
come'? 23He went on:

"You belong to what is below;
I belong to what is above.
You belong to this world—

from verses 22-57. The ball passes from one side to the other, with only oc-
casional editorial comments (vv. 20, 27, 30, 59) to slow up the game.
Whereas chapter 7 disputed the titles of "Christ" and "the prophet" as appli-
cable to Jesus, chapter 8 discusses with passion two different issues. What is
Jesus' relationship to the Father? Is it something so completely different, so
unique, that God is his Father in a way that God is Father to no other
human being? This controversy ranges through the whole of the chapter.
Read for a moment 8:16, 18, 19, 26-27, 28-29, 38, 42, 49, 54. The issue
refuses to stay down or go away. The negative side to it is that if Jesus is the
unique Son of God, what do they become who refuse to believe in him?
They themselves plead that Abraham is their father (vv. 33, 39) and that
through him they are related to God. Jesus' answer is that, though they are
from Abraham's stock (v. 37), they actually deny their family origin by
refusing to do what Abraham did—believe. They turn thereby from the
truth to be believed over to its opposite, a lie engendered by the devil (v.
44). If actions indicate parentage, theirs show the devil as their source, their
father.

a world which cannot hold me.
24 That is why I said you would die in
your sins.
You will surely die in your sins
unless you come to believe that I
AM."
25"Who are you, then?" they asked him.
Jesus answered:
"What I have been telling you from
the beginning.
26 I could say much about you in condemnation,
but no, I only tell the world
what I have heard from him,
the truthful One who sent me."
27They did not grasp that he was speaking to them of the Father. 28Jesus continued:
"When you lift up the Son of Man,
you will come to realize that I AM
and that I do nothing by myself.
I say only what the Father has
taught me.
29 The One who sent me is with me.

He has not deserted me
since I always do what pleases him."
30Because he spoke this way, many came
to believe in him.
Jesus and Abraham. 31Jesus then went
on to say to those Jews who believed in
him:
"If you live according to my teaching,
you are truly my disciples;
32 then you will know the truth,
and the truth will set you free."
33"We are descendants of Abraham," was
their answer. "Never have we been
slaves to anyone. What do you mean by
saying, 'You will be free'?" 34Jesus
answered them:
"I give you my assurance,
everyone who lives in sin
is the slave of sin.
35 (No slave has a permanent place in
the family,
but the son has a place there forever.)

As if this issue were not powerful enough, another raises its head, and this an even more dangerous and troublesome one. Into the chapter comes the majestic designation of the divinity — the awesome, powerful I AM, the *egō eimi*. Used all alone, with neither noun nor adjective to accompany it, as it would be in "I am the good *shepherd*"; "I am *meek* and *humble*," it echoes the divine name found in Isa 41:4; 43:10, 13, 25; 48:12.

In this chapter the form I AM appears three times, in ever increasing clarity:

8:24: "You will surely die in your sins unless you come to believe that I AM."

8:28: "When you lift up the Son of Man, you will come to realize that I AM . . . ."

If these two texts leave some slight doubt about the divine content of the phrase, the final incidence does not:

8:58: "I solemnly declare it: before Abraham came to be, I AM."

Little wonder that "they picked up rocks to throw at Jesus, but he hid himself and slipped out of the temple precincts" (8:59).

³⁶ That is why, if the son frees you, you will really be free.
³⁷ I realize you are of Abraham's stock.
Nonetheless, you are trying to kill me
because my word finds no hearing among you.
³⁸ I tell what I have seen in the Father's presence;
you do what you have heard from your father."
³⁹They retorted, "Our father is Abraham." Jesus told them:
"If you were Abraham's children, you would be following Abraham's example.
⁴⁰ The fact is, you are trying to kill me,
a man who has told you the truth

4. Theological questions and their historical bi-levels. This brief study of chapters 7 and 8 brings to the surface four questions regarding Jesus that were the object of intense and emotional controversy, first during Jesus' lifetime and later during the life of John's Christian community. During the time of Jesus—and later as well, but beginning with Jesus himself—there began the discussion as to whether he was indeed the awaited (a) *Messiah, the Christ,* as also (b) the *prophet like Moses* of whom Deut 18:15, 18 had written. It is this Jesus-level dispute that is apparent in chapter 7—but not in chapter 8. In this latter chapter the questions change, a sign probably that its contents are chronologically later than those of chapter 7. Now the controversy heats up as the issues become even more important. Was, and is, Jesus the (c) *completely unique Son of the Father,* with a relationship so close that he and the Father become identical in will and work and word? Pushing this a step further, can and should Jesus be referred to as (d) *the divine I AM?* Is he God? These two—unique Son and I AM—are the awesome issues of chapter 8 (not of chapter 7). These are also questions, I believe, that originated only after the resurrection of Jesus—questions, then, of John's later community, whose affirmative answers put it in direct and powerful opposition to the Jewish synagogue, within which it had originated.

5. Further comments. This treatment of chapters 7 and 8 is already lengthy, but a few more comments seem required.

a) The reader may have noticed how often Jesus calls himself the one "sent"—sent by the Father, from above, from heaven. Just checking through chapters 7 and 8 brings to evidence ten occurrences: 7:16, 18, 28, 29, 33; 8:16, 18, 26, 29, 42. This word, while implying Jesus' divine origin, also indicates his obedience and subservience to the Father. It will assume a subtle importance in the following chapter.

b) ". . . no one laid a finger on him for *his hour* had not yet come" (7:30). Jesus' "hour" in John is a very specific period of time. At Cana (2:4), as here in 7:30, Jesus' hour is still in the future. We find in 7:39 that the

which I have heard from God.
Abraham did nothing like that.
41 Indeed you are doing your father's
works!"
They cried, "We are no illegitimate
breed! We have but one father and that
is God himself." 42Jesus answered:
"Were God your father
you would love me,
for I came forth from God, and am
here.
I did not come of my own will;
it was he who sent me.
43 Why do you not understand what I
say?
It is because you cannot bear to
hear my word.
44 The father you spring from is the
devil,
and willingly you carry out his
wishes.
He brought death to man from the
beginning,
and has never based himself on
truth;
the truth is not in him.
Lying speech
is his native tongue;
he is a liar and the father of lies.
45 But because I deal in the truth,
you give me no credence.
46 Can any one of you convict me of
sin?
If I am telling the truth,
why do you not believe me?
47 Whoever is of God
hears every word God speaks.

Spirit had not yet been given, "since Jesus had not yet been glorified." The
notions all coalesce. The Spirit will be given when Jesus' hour arrives, which
is the hour of his glorification, of his elevation. In an instance of Johannine
punning, this hour of glorification-elevation begins with the elevation onto
a cross. At that precise moment, as the Son of Man is lifted up, will the
divine I AM be manifested (8:27).

c) I have noted that the special adversaries of Jesus in 8:22-59 are "the
Jews." It is very important for Christians reading, teaching, or especially
preaching from the Fourth Gospel to realize that it can be used to promote
anti-Semitism — and we all have had far too much of that over the centuries
and particularly in our own. There are two points to be made here. One is
that "the Jews" can be contrasted in our Gospel to a whole other segment of
the population that is equally Jewish. Take, for example, 7:13: "No one
dared talk openly about him, however, for fear of *the Jews*." In this context,
all the "no ones" are Jewish people. Who, then, are "the Jews"? As adversaries of Jesus and as contrasted to the people of Jerusalem (7:25-26), they
seem to be clearly identified with the Pharisees of 7:32, 47; with the chief
priests and Pharisees of 7:45; and with the Sanhedrin and Pharisees of 7:48.
Yet even here there are exceptions, as we see in the person of Nicodemus
(7:50-51). In John, consequently, the unfortunate title "the Jews" represents
the authorities, yet not all of them, who by choice and office opposed Jesus
and his teaching. This would be but a small fraction of Jews in Jerusalem, to
say nothing at all of the far greater majority of Jews living away from the
capital city.

The reason you do not hear
is that you are not of God."

⁴⁸The Jews answered, "Are we not right,
after all, in saying you are a Samaritan,
and possessed besides?" ⁴⁹Jesus replied:

"I am not possessed.
However, I revere my Father,
while you fail to respect me.
⁵⁰ I seek no glory for myself;
there is one who seeks it, and it is
he who judges.
⁵¹ I solemnly assure you,
if a man is true to my word
he shall never see death."
⁵²"Now we are sure you are possessed,"
the Jews retorted. "Abraham is dead.
The prophets are dead. Yet you claim,
'A man shall never know death if he
keeps my word.' ⁵³Surely you do not
pretend to be greater than our father
Abraham, who died! Or the prophets,
who died! Whom do you make yourself
out to be?" ⁵⁴Jesus answered:

"If I glorify myself,
that glory comes to nothing.
He who gives me glory is the
Father,
the very one you claim for your
God,
⁵⁵ even though you do not know him.
But I know him.
Were I to say I do not know him,
I would be no better than you—a
liar!
Yes, I know him well,
and I keep his word.
⁵⁶ Your father Abraham rejoiced
that he might see my day.
He saw it and was glad."

⁵⁷At this the Jews objected: "You are not
yet fifty! How can you have seen Abraham?" ⁵⁸Jesus answered them:

"I solemnly declare it:
before Abraham came to be, I AM."

⁵⁹At that they picked up rocks to throw
at Jesus, but he hid himself and slipped
out of the temple precincts.

The second point is that by the time John is writing this Gospel, a change
has occurred. Christians have come into existence. The majority would now
be Gentile, but even Jewish Christians will have assumed their own Christian identity and been separated from their previous Jewish society. Contact
between Jewish Christians and non-Christians has moved from tolerance to
discussion to controversy to angry separation and excommunication. In this
sorry evolution, the term "the Jews," which in Jesus' day represented just a
small body of in-family adversaries, can be used to represent the Jews as a
whole, resistant to Christian belief. This was a pitiable development,
perhaps inevitable; but the ill feelings of John's time will be thoroughly immoral if perpetuated in our own century. The long and heavy legacy of hate
and murder that has piled up over the centuries must be attacked with a
peculiarly Johannine weapon—that of love.

d) Critical readers will have already noticed that nothing has been said
thus far about 8:1-11, the account of the woman taken in adultery. In
modern editions of the Fourth Gospel, this passage is ordinarily either
dropped into the footnotes or placed within brackets to indicate that it is
not part of John's original text. It is missing from our oldest and best Greek
manuscripts and seems to have been unknown to the early Greek Fathers,

since they did not comment on it. In various old manuscripts it is found either at 8:1, as in our text, or after 7:36, or at the end of the Gospel, or after Luke 21:38. The earliest certain reference to the story is found in a third-century writing on church discipline called the *Didascalia*. In a word, it did not form part of the original Gospel of John.

Notwithstanding the mystery of the story's transmission, and of its insertion into John (because of 8:15?), it contains one of the most striking portrayals of Jesus' mercy and is a strong plea for its own authenticity. It possesses all the signs of historical truth. It must be a story dating back to Jesus that was passed along by oral tradition and used, perhaps, to solve the problem of forgiveness of sin for baptized Christians. It sounds incredibly like a Lukan narrative, dealing as it does with mercy, sin, and a woman.

One of the questions always asked about this beautiful passage is what Jesus was writing on the ground. Two reasonably plausible suggestions are that the doodling indicated lack of interest or that John wished to refer to the Greek text of Jer 17:13: ". . . may those who turn away from thee *be written on the earth*, for they have forsaken the fountain of life, the Lord."

e) The light and water aspects of the Jewish feast of Booths manifest themselves in the significant reference to the living water of the Spirit in 7:37-39, and to Jesus as light of the world in 8:12. It is to that last notion that John will turn his attention in the following chapter.

9:1–10:42 Episode V: Light of the World, Sight and Blindness

This fifth episode focuses on light, on Jesus as the light of the world (prepared for in 8:12), which light can bring sight to those previously blind as well as blindness to those who, confident in their own sight, turn away from the light. The episode does not stop with chapter 9 but continues on into and through chapter 10. It includes three sections: the man born blind (ch. 9); the good shepherd (10:1-21); the feast of Hanukkah (10:22-42). The sections are linked together. Verse 10:21 connects the good shepherd segment to the man born blind, and 10:26-28 connects the Hanukkah segment to that of the good shepherd.

1. The man born blind (9:1-41). We have spoken already of dramatic elements in John: of the technique of ambiguity, misunderstanding, clarification; of dramatic progression of knowledge in the case of the Samaritan woman; of characters, historical though they be, who also have dramatic roles to play, like the "missionary figures" of Andrew and Philip. Chapter 9 is undoubtedly the most dramatic of John's Gospel, and we would like to demonstrate this to an extent by laying it out, word for word from the text, but with the verses divided among various readers as it might be on the stage. Pass out the parts, and *voilà*, instant theater!

[SCENE 1]

Disciples: [1]As he walked along, he saw a man who had been blind from birth. [2]His disciples asked him, "Rabbi, was it his sin or that of his parents that caused him to be born blind?"

Jesus: [3]"Neither," answered Jesus. "It was no sin, either of this man or of his parents. Rather, it was to let God's works show forth in him. [4]We must do the deeds of him who sent me while it is day. The night comes on when no one can work. [5]While I am in the world I am the light of the world."

[6]With that, Jesus spat on the ground, made mud with his saliva, and smeared the man's eyes with the mud. [7]Then he told him, "Go, wash in the pool of Siloam." (This name means "One who has been sent.")

Blind Man: So the man went off and washed, and came back able to see.

[SCENE 2]

Neighbor 1: [8]His neighbors and the people who had been accustomed to see him begging began to ask, "Isn't this the fellow who used to sit and beg?"

Neighbor 2: [9]Some were claiming it was he;

Neighbor 3: others maintained it was not but someone who looked like him.

Blind Man: The man himself said, "I am the one."

Neighbor 1: [10]They said to him then,

Neighbor 1-2-3: "How were your eyes opened?"

Blind Man: [11]He answered, "That man they call Jesus made mud and smeared it on my eyes, telling me to go to Siloam and wash. When I did go and wash, I was able to see."

Neighbor 1-2-3: [12]"Where is he?"

Neighbor 1: they asked.

Blind Man: He replied, "I have no idea."

[SCENE 3]

Pharisee 1: [13]Next, they took the man who had been born blind to the Pharisees. [14]Note that it was on a sabbath that Jesus had made the mud paste and opened his eyes. [15]The Pharisees, in turn, began to inquire how he had recovered his sight.

Blind Man: He told them, "He put mud on my eyes. I washed it off, and now I can see."

Pharisee 2: [16]This prompted some of the Pharisees to assert, "This man cannot be from God because he does not keep the sabbath."

Pharisee 3: Others objected, "If a man is a sinner, how can he perform signs like these?"

Pharisee 1: They were sharply divided over him. [17]Then they addressed the blind man again:

Pharisee 1-2-3: "Since it was your eyes he opened, what do you have to say about him?"

Blind Man: "He is a prophet," he replied.

[SCENE 4]

Authorities 1: [18]The Jews refused to believe that he had really been born blind and had begun to see, until they summoned the parents of this man who now could see.

Authorities 2: [19]"Is this your son?" they asked, "and if so, do you attest that he was blind at birth? How do you account for the fact that now he can see?"

Parent 1: [20]The parents answered:

Parent 2: "We know this is our son, and we know he was blind at birth. [21]But how he can see now, or who opened his eyes, we have no idea. Ask him. He is old enough to speak for himself."

Parent 1: [22](His parents answered in this fashion because they were afraid of the Jews, who had already agreed among themselves that anyone who acknowledged Jesus as the Messiah would be put out of the synagogue. [23]That was why his parents said,

Parent 2: "He is of age — ask him.")

[SCENE 5]

Authorities 1: [24]A second time they summoned the man who had been born blind and said to him, "Give glory to God! First of all, we know this man is a sinner."

Blind Man: [25]"I do not know whether he is a sinner or not," he answered. "I know this much: I was blind before; now I can see."

Authorities 2: [26]They persisted: "Just what did he do to you? How did he open your eyes?"

Blind Man: [27]"I have told you once, but you would not listen to me," he answered them. "Why do you want to hear it all over again? Do not tell me you want to become his disciples too?"

Authorities 3: [28]They retorted scornfully: "You are the one who is that man's disciple. We are disciples of Moses. [29]We know that God spoke to Moses, but we have no idea where this man comes from."

Blind Man: [30]He came back at them: "Well, this is news! You do not know where he comes from, yet he opened my eyes. [31]We know that God does not hear sinners, but that if someone is devout and obeys his will, he listens to him. [32]It is unheard of that anyone ever gave sight to a person blind from birth. [33]If this man were not from God, he could never have done such a thing."

Authorities 1: [34]"What!" they exclaimed,

Authorities 2: "You are steeped in sin from your birth, and you are giving us lectures?"

Authorities 1-2-3: With that they threw him out bodily.

[SCENE 6]

Jesus: [35]When Jesus heard of his expulsion, he sought him out and asked him, "Do you believe in the Son of Man?"

Blind Man: [36]He answered, "Who is he, sir, that I may believe in him?"

Jesus: [37]"You have seen him," Jesus replied. "He is speaking to you now."

Blind Man: [38]"I do believe, Lord," he said, and bowed down to worship him.

Jesus: [39]Then Jesus said: "I came into this world to divide it, to make the sightless see and the seeing blind."

Pharisee 1: [40]Some of the Pharisees around him picked this up, saying,

Pharisees 1-2-3: "You are not calling us the blind, are you?"

Jesus: [41]To which Jesus replied: "If you were blind there would be no sin in that. 'But we see,' you say, and your sin remains."

The preceding lay-out makes the dramatic pattern of the chapter clear. There are six logically successive scenes; brilliant dialogue; characters that are, in turn, merciful, confused, strong, bullying, weak, and self-interested. Playing the major role — even upstaging Jesus — is the intriguing figure of the blind man, courageous and intelligent, counter-punching with success every blow thrown his way. And the play closes with a fine line (v. 41) that gives the gist of the whole story.

The account demands little or no explanation of small details. What is all-important is to capture the deep, underlying truths that our evangelical dramatist has written into it.

a) The story has undoubtedly been used for baptismal instruction. The reader will have noted the happy coincidence of the *blind* man *washing* in a *pool* called *Siloam*, which means *sent*. Having already noted (Episode IV, 5 [a]) that "sent" is a veritable nickname for Jesus in the Fourth Gospel, we can be certain that John is writing of the physical cure in such a way that it reflects and calls to mind the cure of spiritual blindness — from birth — granted to those who wash sacramentally in the pool that is truly Jesus, the "sent one." (It is not hard to imagine that the effect of baptism was explained to catechumens as the immersion in Christ that would provide the insight of reality to which they had been blind from birth.)

Speaking in the same vein, the blind man's progressive enlightenment parallels the progress in knowledge that the catechumens would have followed as they were instructed in the faith. From first knowledge of the fact that there was a man called Jesus (v. 11), they would have advanced to deeper insights into his character as prophet (v. 17), as man from God (v. 33), as the heavenly Son of Man (v. 35), culminating in the final act of worship of Jesus as Lord (v. 38). This progression reflects not only the steps of the catechumen toward complete faith but also an enlivening dramatic technique on the part of the evangelist.

b) The passage is rich in irony, another dramatic touch. The reality of things is just the opposite of what it seems to be. Those who are sure they can see are, in truth, blind, and are so by their own choosing (vv. 40-41). He who starts out blind takes a risk at Jesus' invitation (v. 6) and ends up seeing. He passes from blindness to sight to insight. He is a striking example of the deep theology of which his cure is a *sign*. Jesus is indeed the LIGHT OF THE WORLD (v. 5). The sad foils to this man cured of both blindness and ignorance are the neighbors, who remain in ignorance (vv. 8-12); the parents, who refuse to take a risk — "He is of age, ask him" (v. 23); the Pharisees, who cannot make up their collective minds (vv. 13-17); and the authorities and Pharisees, who refuse to believe what their eyes see (vv. 24,

The Good Shepherd

10 ¹"Truly I assure you:
Whoever does not enter the
sheepfold through the gate
but climbs in some other way
is a thief and a marauder.

² The one who enters through the
gate
is shepherd of the sheep;
³ the keeper opens the gate for him.
The sheep hear his voice
as he calls his own by name
and leads them out.

40). No one is so blind as the person who refuses to see. "If you were blind there would be no sin in that. 'But we see,' you say, and your sin remains" (v. 41).

c) We find in this chapter the most outstanding example in John of the use of historical bi-levels. The Jesus-level of the cure of the blind has been subtly interpenetrated by the later historical level of John's own community experience. The revealing element in this compenetration is the statement in verse 22 that "anyone who acknowledged Jesus as the Messiah would be put out of the synagogue." And, of course, the cured man was thrown out (v. 34). Such excommunication from the synagogue because of belief in Jesus was not a feature of Jesus' lifetime, nor even of Paul's, whose final trip to Jerusalem found him worshiping in the temple (Acts 21:26). But the relationship between Jewish Christians and the synagogue soured over the decades, and especially with the increasing Christian insight that Jesus was truly God, truly the I AM. Eventually the synagogue prayer was enlarged to include a curse of such heretics as the Christians. No Jewish Christian could, of course, share such a prayer, and that resulted effectively in the excommunication of Jewish Christians.

This whole Gospel, and chapter 9 in particular, reflects this historical crisis. John and his fellow Jewish Christians are angry. They have been thrown out (v. 34). Part of the reason for including this chapter in the Gospel was to strengthen those who had undergone this trauma. Expelled from synagogue, family, and friends as heretics, they were encouraged by this account to fall at the feet of the Lord to worship him (v. 38).

2. The good shepherd (10:1-21). The first question to tackle here is why this section is in this position. Why does it follow the story of the man born blind? There appears to be no connection between 9:41 and 10:1; rather, 10:1 introduces abruptly the shepherd theme, which is totally unexpected after the material of chapter 9. This difficulty has again led some scholars to move chapter 10 to another place in the Gospel. It is, they say, a displacement. Yet it need not be and probably is not. The reference to the cure of the blind in verse 21 ties this segment to the preceding chapter. More to the point, the discussion about the sheep and the shepherd is probably being used by John as a statement regarding the miserable shepherding being ef-

⁴ When he has brought out [all] those
   that are his,
he walks in front of them,
and the sheep follow him
because they recognize his voice.

⁵ They will not follow a stranger;
such a one they will flee,
because they do not recognize a
   stranger's voice."

⁶Even though Jesus used this figure with
them, they did not grasp what he was
trying to tell them. ⁷He therefore said [to
them again]:

"My solemn word is this:
I am the sheepgate.

⁸ All who came before me
were thieves and marauders

whom the sheep did not heed.

⁹ I am the gate.
Whoever enters through me
will be safe.
He will go in and out,
and find pasture.

¹⁰ The thief comes
only to steal and slaughter and destroy.
I came
that they might have life
and have it to the full.

¹¹ I am the good shepherd;
the good shepherd lays down his life
for the sheep.

¹² The hired hand—who is no shepherd
nor owner of the sheep—

fected by such authorities as appear in the case of the man born blind. Blind guides themselves, they not only fail to recognize the leading light that is Jesus but cast out of the synagogue the one man who does accept the light. Verse 6 insists that they still just do not understand.

Crucial to the identification of the author's purpose at this point is the necessary realization that he is writing about Jesus with the text of Ezek 34 in clear view. In that passage, Ezekiel, speaking God's word, excoriates the authorities of his own time. They had become irresponsible and thieving shepherds, feeding themselves rather than their flock. So God would take away their maladministration and become the shepherd himself. Finally he would appoint another shepherd after the figure of David. John sees all of this coming true in Jesus. God has become the shepherd in Jesus, himself Messiah and Son of David. Jesus' fidelity to his sheep, his sacrifice for them, stands out in contrast to the failure of the stumbling, blinded, bullying authorities in chapter 9.

Metaphors come fast and often in these verses. There are the sheep— easily identified as the flock that Jesus intends to lead into good pasture (v. 9), those whom he knows by name and who recognize his voice (vv. 3-4, 14), those whom he intends to defend against thieves and marauders (vv. 1, 8, 10) and whom he wishes to join together with all others who, listening to his voice, will come into the one fold (v. 16). Jesus will effect all this because he is the GOOD SHEPHERD (vv. 11, 14), loved by the Father because *he will lay down his life for the sheep*. It is this act of total, loving self-sacrifice that is mentioned again and again as the central motif. Appearing first in verse 11 as the good shepherd title is introduced, it occurs again in verses

catches sight of the wolf coming
and runs away, leaving the sheep
to be snatched and scattered by the
wolf.
13 That is because he works for pay;
he has no concern for the sheep.
14 "I am the good shepherd.
I know my sheep
and my sheep know me
15 in the same way that the Father
knows me
and I know the Father;
for these sheep I will give my life.
16 I have other sheep
that do not belong to this fold.
I must lead them, too,
and they shall hear my voice.
There shall be one flock then, one
shepherd.

17 The Father loves me for this:
that I lay down my life
to take it up again.
18 No one takes it from me;
I lay it down freely.
I have power to lay it down,
and I have power to take it up again.
This command I received from my
Father."

19Because of these words, the Jews were
sharply divided once more. 20Many were
claiming: "He is possessed by a
devil — out of his mind! Why pay any attention to him?" 21Others maintained:
"These are not the words of a madman.
Surely a devil cannot open the eyes of
the blind!"

Feast of the Dedication. 22It was
winter, and the time came for the feast

15, 17, and twice in verse 18. Though the shepherd-sheep metaphor was
well known in the Old Testament Scriptures (as in Ezek 34), this laying
down of the shepherd's life is something new. It is the characteristic function
of Jesus. He is the good shepherd especially because of his willing self-
sacrifice.

A final metaphor is that of the gate (vv. 7, 9), also applied to Jesus. He it
is who provides safety for the flock by prohibiting entrance to marauders
and who provides food by opening out onto good pasture lands. That the
two metaphors of shepherd and sheepgate do not co-exist easily may be a
sign that they originated separately but have been brought together here for
this chapter.

In these verses we have seen two more of John's I AM — plus a following
noun — statements. Jesus, who has identified himself as "I am the bread of
life" (6:35, 41, 51) and "I am the light of the world" (8:12; 9:5), now says, "I
am the sheepgate . . . the gate" (vv. 7, 9) and "I am the good shepherd" (vv.
11, 14). And since Jesus is the incarnate-Word revelation of the Father, we
recognize in these personal characteristics of the Lord the same loving
features of the Father.

Such revelation, as always, is followed by a crisis of faith. Is Jesus a
possessed madman or just the opposite? Whose power is it that opens the
eyes of the blind (vv. 19-21)?

3. The feast of Hanukkah. This feast celebrated the reconsecration of the
temple by Judas the Maccabean (164 b.c.) after its profanation three years
earlier by the Syrian Antiochus IV Epiphanes (1 Macc 4:36-59; 2 Macc

of the Dedication in Jerusalem. ²³Jesus was walking in the temple area, in Solomon's Portico, ²⁴when the Jews gathered around him and said, "How long are you going to keep us in suspense? If you really are the Messiah, tell us so in plain words." ²⁵Jesus answered:

"I did tell you, but you do not believe.

The works I do in my Father's name give witness in my favor,

²⁶ but you refuse to believe because you are not my sheep.

²⁷ My sheep hear my voice. I know them, and they follow me.

²⁸ I give them eternal life, and they shall never perish.

No one shall snatch them out of my hand.

²⁹ My Father is greater than all, in what he has given me, and there is no snatching out of his hand.

³⁰ The Father and I are one."

³¹When some of the Jews again reached for rocks to stone him, ³²Jesus protested to them, "Many good deeds have I shown you from the Father. For which of these do you stone me?" ³³"It is not for any 'good deed' that we are stoning you," the Jews retorted, "but for blaspheming. You who are only a man are making yourself God." ³⁴Jesus answered:

"Is it not written in your law,

10:1-8). This yearly celebration lasted nine days, was a "lights" ceremony like the feast of Tabernacles (7:2), and was celebrated in mid-December. "It was winter" (v. 22). The scene for the present incident in John is set "in Solomon's Portico," a colonnade on the east side of the temple overlooking the Kidron Valley. It was a favorite rendezvous for Christians in Acts 3:11–4:4; 5:12, where it also appears as a place of controversy between Jewish Christians and some of their fellow Jews. Material from such a subsequent argument may well have entered into these verses.

The substance of the dialogue (vv. 24-38) is quite similar to that of chapters 7–8. One question at issue is whether Jesus is the Messiah (v. 24), a possible editorial link to the David figure of Ezek 34, which stood in the background of the preceding section. The other question is whether Jesus is the unique Son of God, whether God is in a very unique way *his Father*. In this brief section, "Father" appears nine times (vv. 25, 29 [twice], 30, 32, 36, 37, 38 [twice]); and "God's Son" is Jesus' claim in verse 36. What more can he offer as proof than his works done through the Father, works that are themselves the Father's revealing words? But Jesus' adversaries will not believe, as Jesus' divine works indicate, that he and the Father are one (v. 30), that the Father is in him and he in the Father (v. 38).

At one point Jesus almost plays with his opponents over the unique-Son-of-God issue. If Ps 82:6 calls judges "gods" because they share in the divine work of judgment, why should people object if Jesus is called "Son of God," since the Father has consecrated him and sent him into the world (vv. 34-36)? To this do the works testify. The incident ends on a sad note: "They again tried to arrest him, but he eluded their grasp" (v. 39).

'I have said, You are gods'?
35 If it calls those men gods
to whom God's word was addressed—
and Scripture cannot lose its force—
36 do you claim that I blasphemed
when, as he whom the Father consecrated
and sent into the world,
I said, 'I am God's Son'?
37 If I do not perform my Father's
works,
put no faith in me.
38 But if I do perform them,
even though you put no faith in me,
put faith in these works,
so as to realize what it means
that the Father is in me
and I in him."

39At these words they again tried to arrest him, but he eluded their grasp.
Return to the Jordan. 40Then he went
back across the Jordan to the place
where John had been baptizing earlier,
and while he stayed there 41many people
came to him. "John may never have performed a sign," they commented, "but
whatever John said about this man was
true." 42In that place, many came to
believe in him.

11 **The Raising of Lazarus.** 1There
was a certain man named Lazarus
who was sick. He was from Bethany, the
village of Mary and her sister Martha.
2(This Mary whose brother Lazarus was
sick was the one who anointed the Lord
with perfume and dried his feet with her
hair.) 3The sisters sent word to Jesus to

The final verses (40–42) are a brief presentation of the other side of Jesus'
mission. Many came to him, accepted the witness of his signs and of John's
testimony (a final reference to the Baptist), and came to believe in him. This
paragraph also begins to position Jesus for his move to Bethany (ch. 11)
and, in triumph, to Jerusalem (v. 12).

One final observation may be of value. John may well have intended a
linkage between Jesus as the one "whom the Father *consecrated* and sent
into the world" (10:36) and the feast of the Dedication (v. 22), a memorial of
the temple's *consecration* after Syrian profanation. If so, this is another in a
line of attempts by John to show how Jesus had replaced the Jewish institu-
tions. We have seen (1) how Jesus replaced *the temple* (2:13-22); (2) how he
is a veritable *Lord of the sabbath*, working as does his Father (5:16-18); (3)
how at *Passover* (ch. 6) he gives and becomes the manna bread and saves
from the water; (4) how in chapters 7–8 at *Tabernacles* he is the living water
and the light of the world. And now (5) Jesus replaces *Hanukkah*. He is the
consecrated one. As John writes, the temple has disappeared, and Jewish
Christians have been expelled from the synagogues. Fear not, says John,
Jesus himself is sufficient to replace all these lost and precious treasures.

11:1-54 Episode VI: Life over Death

Jesus is both resurrection and life (11:25), and the restoration of Lazarus
is the sign. John has already introduced us to the "life theme" when speaking
in Episode I of rebirth (Nicodemus) and living water (Samaritan woman); in

inform him, "Lord, the one you love is sick." ⁴Upon hearing this, Jesus said:

"This sickness is not to end in death;
rather it is for God's glory,
that through it the Son of God may
be glorified."

⁵Jesus loved Martha and her sister and Lazarus very much. ⁶Yet, after hearing that Lazarus was sick, he stayed on where he was for two days more. ⁷Finally he said to his disciples, "Let us go back to Judea." ⁸"Rabbi," protested the disciples, "with the Jews only recently trying to stone you, you are going back up there again?" ⁹Jesus answered:

"Are there not twelve hours of daylight?
If a man goes walking by day he
does not stumble
because he sees the world bathed in
light.
¹⁰ But if he goes walking at night he
will stumble
since there is no light in him."

¹¹After uttering these words, he added, "Our beloved Lazarus has fallen asleep, but I am going there to wake him." ¹²At this the disciples objected, "Lord, if he is asleep his life will be saved." ¹³Jesus had been speaking about his death, but they thought he meant sleep in the sense of slumber. ¹⁴Finally Jesus said plainly: "Lazarus is dead. ¹⁵For your sakes I am glad I was not there, that you may come to believe. In any event, let us go to him." ¹⁶Then Thomas (the name means "Twin") said to his fellow disciples, "Let us go along, to die with him."

¹⁷When Jesus arrived at Bethany, he found that Lazarus had already been in the tomb four days. ¹⁸The village was not far from Jerusalem—just under two miles—¹⁹and many Jewish people had come out to console Martha and Mary over their brother. ²⁰When Martha heard that Jesus was coming she went to meet him, while Mary sat at home. ²¹Martha said to Jesus, "Lord, if you had been here, my brother would never have

Episode II's life-giving word; in Episode III's life-giving bread; in Episode IV's "light of life" (8:12); in Episode V's "I have come that they might have life and have it to the full" (10:10).

Our present episode concentrates on this theme in one well-organized presentation, again one that adapts easily to theater. Pass out the roles—the sisters, Jesus, the disciples and Thomas, Jews/authorities and Caiaphas, a narrator—and the stage is set. It is drama with constant motion. The message of distress goes *from Bethany near Jerusalem* (v. 18) *to Jesus*, a message so simple and trusting that it might well become ours when friends are ill: "Lord, the one you love is sick" (v. 3). Jesus and his disciples move *toward Bethany*. Martha and Mary move *to Jesus*. All move *to the tomb*. Lazarus moves *out of the tomb*. Informers move *to the Pharisees*. Jesus and his company move *to Ephraim* in northern Judea.

Mary and her sister Martha are known to us also from the Martha and Mary story in Luke 10:38-42. The personality characterizations are similar in both Luke and John. Martha comes through as the more dominant and active. It is she who is so busy in Luke 10:40 and who moves rapidly at first notice to meet Jesus here in John 11:20. Mary sat at home and later fell at Jesus' feet (John 11:20, 32); in Luke 10:39 she also sat at the Lord's feet to

died. ²²Even now, I am sure that God will give you whatever you ask of him." ²³"Your brother will rise again," Jesus assured her. ²⁴"I know he will rise again," Martha replied, "in the resurrection on the last day." ²⁵Jesus told her:

"I am the resurrection and the life:
²⁶ whoever believes in me,
though he should die, will come to life;
and whoever is alive and believes in me
will never die.
Do you believe this?" ²⁷"Yes, Lord," she replied. "I have come to believe that you are the Messiah, the Son of God: he who is to come into the world."

²⁸When she had said this she went back and called her sister Mary. "The Teacher is here, asking for you," she whispered. ²⁹As soon as Mary heard this, she got up and started out in his direction. ³⁰(Actually Jesus had not yet come into the village but was still at the spot where Martha had met him.) ³¹The Jews who were in the house with Mary consoling her saw her get up quickly and go out, so they followed her, thinking she was going to the tomb to weep there. ³²When Mary came to the place where

listen to his words. Surprisingly, Luke says nothing about a brother Lazarus, though he does present a parable regarding Lazarus, the poor man who ends up in Abraham's bosom. The Lukan story ends with the provocative conclusion: "If they do not listen to Moses and the prophets, they will not be convinced even if one should rise from the dead" (Luke 16:31). This is not meant to insinuate that John has turned the Lazarus of the parable into the brother of Mary and Martha. His characters are real people, and his knowledge of Jerusalem and its environs—which includes Bethany—is trustworthy.

What is truly touching about this incident is the author's insistence on the deep love that Jesus felt for this small family group, within which he must have felt so much at home. This love is evident in verses 5, 11, 35-36. Since Lazarus is the only male disciple of whom Jesus' love is predicated in the Gospel, some commentators have suggested that he is the beloved disciple who will become prominent in our later chapters. This is not probable, since the evangelist goes out of his way to preserve the anonymity of this central character.

There is some evidence that this Lazarus story was a second-edition addend to John's Gospel. This would explain the otherwise odd reference in verse 2 to the anointing by Mary, which will occur only in the following chapter. The oddness would disappear if the author had already included chapter 12 in his first edition and could thus allude to it when adding on what was to become chapter 11.

Our story is rich in the theology it unfolds.

1) Verses 25-26 are the theological center of the whole chapter. Jesus is both the resurrection and the life for all who, like Martha, believe that he is "the Messiah, the Son of God" (v. 27, the same profession that will be found

Jesus was, seeing him, she fell at his feet and said to him, "Lord, if you had been here my brother would never have died." ³³When Jesus saw her weeping, and the Jews who had accompanied her also weeping, he was troubled in spirit, moved by the deepest emotions. ³⁴"Where have you laid him?" he asked. "Lord, come and see," they said. ³⁵Jesus began to weep, ³⁶which caused the Jews to remark, "See how much he loved him!" ³⁷But some said, "He opened the eyes of that blind man. Why could he not have done something to stop this man from dying?" ³⁸Once again troubled in spirit, Jesus approached the tomb.

It was a cave with a stone laid across it. ³⁹"Take away the stone," Jesus directed. Martha, the dead man's sister, said to him, "Lord, It has been four days now; surely there will be a stench!" ⁴⁰Jesus replied, "Did I not assure you that if you believed you would see the glory of God displayed?" ⁴¹They then took away the stone and Jesus looked upward and said:

"Father, I thank you for having heard me.

⁴² I know that you always hear me but I have said this for the sake of the crowd, that they may believe that you sent me."

⁴³Having said this he called loudly, "Lazarus, come out!" ⁴⁴The dead man

in 20:31). One who has faith, even after death, shall live; one who has faith and is alive will never really die. Of this the restoration of Lazarus is the sign.

2) We find here a stunning example of Jesus' *life-giving word* and are reminded of the sayings in Episode II: "I solemnly assure you, an hour is coming, has indeed come, when the dead shall hear the voice of the Son of God, and those who have heeded it shall live. . . . an hour is coming in which all those in their tombs shall hear his voice and come forth" (John 5:25, 28).

3) John's salvation theology is voiced in the unintentional prophecy of Caiaphas. "Jesus would die for the nation — and not for this nation only, but to gather into one all the dispersed children of God" (vv. 51-52).

4) Deeply hidden in the episode is a further truth: that Jesus' gift of life to Lazarus involves his own death, the offering of his own life. To love Lazarus and give him life, Jesus must be willing to risk and lose his own. This trip to Bethany is shadowed by the approaching cross (vv. 7-8, 16, 50-53).

It is remarkable how the account of Lazarus' resurrection parallels that of Jesus himself in chapter 20. Both accounts speak of:
 — a mourning Mary at the tomb (11:31 and 20:11);
 — a cave tomb closed with a stone (11:38, 41 and 20:1);
 — grave clothes plus a face cloth (11:44 and 20:6-7);
 — a special role given to Thomas (11:16 and 20:24-28).
John has written the story of Lazarus in such a way as to prefigure Jesus' resurrection. Chapter 11 is meant to prepare the reader for chapter 20.

came out, bound hand and foot with linen strips, his face wrapped in a cloth. "Untie him," Jesus told them, "and let him go free."

Session of the Sanhedrin. ⁴⁵This caused many of the Jews who had come to visit Mary, and had seen what Jesus did, to put their faith in him. ⁴⁶Some others, however, went to the Pharisees and reported what Jesus had done. ⁴⁷The result was that the chief priests and the Pharisees called a meeting of the Sanhedrin. "What are we to do," they said, "with this man performing all sorts of signs? ⁴⁸If we let him go on like this, the whole world will believe in him. Then the Romans will come in and sweep away our sanctuary and our nation." ⁴⁹One of their number named Caiaphas, who was high priest that year, addressed them at this point: "You have no understanding whatever! ⁵⁰Can you not see that it is better for you to have one man die [for the people] than to have the whole nation destroyed?" ⁵¹(He did not say this on his own. It was rather as high priest for that year that he prophesied that Jesus would die for the nation— ⁵²and not for this nation only, but to gather into one all the dispersed children of God.)

⁵³From that day onward there was a plan afoot to kill him. ⁵⁴In consequence, Jesus no longer moved about freely in Jewish circles. He withdrew instead to a town called Ephraim in the region near the desert, where he stayed with his disciples.

The Last Passover. ⁵⁵The Jewish Passover was near, which meant that many people from the country went up to Jerusalem for Passover purification.

We conclude this chapter with a few minor observations. We must be struck by the unexpected delay on the part of Jesus in verses 4-7. Why didn't Jesus prevent the death rather than wait to overcome it? Our author looks at the event from the divine viewpoint rather than the human, and it is this that is promoted by Jesus' words in verses 4, 9, and 15. John, *looking back at the incident,* can now see, and have Jesus proclaim, that it was all for the better. The miracle sign has evidenced God's glory, his presence, and in the person of the Son of God. The miracle was an epiphany. The God of healing love is revealed through the work of his Son. And it is through walking with this Son, himself the light of this world (thus reads the Greek text hidden in our translation, "the world bathed in light" of verse 9), that we are assured of not stumbling.

Caiaphas, whose words unintentionally become so theological in the final verses, was high priest for some nineteen years, from about A.D. 18–37. He was the son-in-law of Annas.

The final verses of the episode (53-54) position Jesus in Ephraim near the desert. From there he will ascend a last time to Bethany and Jerusalem.

11:55–12:50 Episode VII: Life Through Death

This final episode in the Book of Signs will teach not only that Jesus overcomes death (as in the Lazarus story) but that he will give life precisely through death. The text is divided into six clearly distinct but intercon-

⁵⁶They were on the lookout for Jesus, various people in the temple vicinity saying to each other, "What do you think? Is he likely to come for the feast?" ⁵⁷(The chief priests and the Pharisees had given orders that anyone who knew where he was should report it, so that they could apprehend him.)

12 Anointing at Bethany. ¹Six days before Passover Jesus came to Bethany, the village of Lazarus whom Jesus had raised from the dead. ²There they gave him a banquet, at which Martha served. Lazarus was one of those at table with him. ³Mary brought a pound of costly perfume made from genuine aromatic nard, with which she anointed Jesus' feet. Then she dried his feet with her hair, and the house was filled with the ointment's fragrance. ⁴Judas Iscariot, one of his disciples (the one about to hand him over), protested: ⁵"Why was not this perfume sold? It could have brought three hundred silver pieces, and the money have been given to the poor." ⁶(He did not say this out of concern for the poor, but because he was a thief. He held the purse, and used to help himself to what was deposited there.) ⁷To this Jesus replied: "Leave her alone. Let her keep it against the day they prepare me for burial. ⁸The poor you always have with you, but me you will not always have."

nected segments: the introduction; the anointing; the triumphal entry; Jesus' hour; the evangelist's evaluation; Jesus' summary proclamation.

1. Introduction (11:55-57). Our initial verse is almost identical to 6:4, which also introduces Passover material. The double mention of the Passover (v. 55) will lead us naturally into 12:1. The scene is being set as people wonder aloud whether or not Jesus is coming. Meanwhile (v. 57), the trap, too, is being set.

2. The anointing (12:1-11). As we move into material concerning the passion, we find that John's Gospel becomes much more similar to the other three. This story of the anointing, for example, resembles closely that of Mark 14:1-11 and Matt 26:1-16. (Luke 7:36-50 also has an anointing incident, but its time frame and purpose are quite different.) Although Martha, Mary, and Lazarus are prominent, the text definitely avoids saying that the meal was given at their home. Mark and Matthew place it in the home of Simon the leper. John does not disagree.

It is interesting to read, and it seems so correct, that "Martha served" while Mary "anointed Jesus' feet" (vv. 2-3). The protest by Judas Iscariot allows the evangelist to put at center stage for just a moment this disciple who will be the tragic figure in the drama beginning to unfold. He steals from the poor; eventually he will lose his all. The key expression in this narrative, however, is that of Jesus in verse 7: "Let her keep it against the day they prepare me for *burial.*" The ointment is not simply cosmetic perfume; it is not simply preparation for death; it is burial ointment and fills the house with fragrance just as the scent of funeral oils pervades a tomb. This burial motif will surface again shortly.

⁹The great crowd of Jews discovered he was there and came out, not only because of Jesus but also to see Lazarus, whom he had raised from the dead. ¹⁰The fact was, the chief priests planned to kill Lazarus too, ¹¹because many Jews were going over to Jesus and believing in him on account of Lazarus.

Entry into Jerusalem. ¹²The next day the great crowd that had come for the feast heard that Jesus was to enter Jerusalem, ¹³so they got palm branches and came out to meet him. They kept shouting:

"Hosanna!
Blessed is he who comes in the name of the Lord!
Blessed is the king of Israel!"

¹⁴Jesus found a donkey and mounted it, in accord with Scripture:

¹⁵ "Fear not, O daughter of Zion!
Your king approaches you
on a donkey's colt."

¹⁶(At first, the disciples did not understand all this, but after Jesus was glorified they recalled that the people had done to him precisely what had been written about him.) ¹⁷The crowd that was present when he called Lazarus out of the tomb and raised him from the dead kept testifying to it. ¹⁸The crowd came out to meet him because they heard he had performed this sign. ¹⁹The Pharisees remarked to one another, "See, there is nothing you can do! The whole world has run after him."

The Coming of Jesus' Hour. ²⁰Among those who had come up to worship at the feast were some Greeks. ²¹They ap-

With verse 9 the "great crowd" moves onto the scene. It will remain throughout, and for a purpose that will appear in just a moment. But for now Lazarus is featured. The authorities plan to have him, like so many later disciples, share Jesus' fate. His very existence is too strong a proof of Jesus' life-giving word.

3. The triumphal entry (12:12-19). The crowd takes over this scene (vv. 12, 17, 18) as Jesus enters Jerusalem one last time. He comes as king (vv. 13, 15), a motif that will become very strong in the passion account. The exultant prayer of verse 13 originates from Ps 118:25-26, a psalm used regularly by pilgrims entering the Holy City. To it is joined a post-resurrection application (v. 15) of Zech 9:9. Zechariah's king, like John's, is humble. Though victorious, he rides, not the stallion of war, but the donkey of service. The crowds that introduce the scene (v. 12) are in strong evidence at its conclusion (vv. 17, 18), where their presence provokes the Pharisees' reaction. Jesus' gift of life to Lazarus is going to demand a frightening exchange: Jesus' life for that of his friend. This segment concludes with the important phrasing: "The whole world has run after him" (v. 19). Part of this world is the Jewish crowd that we have observed repeatedly.

4. Jesus' hour (12:20-36). This section—a combination of narrative, monologue, and dialogue—is the key to the whole chapter. It follows one narrative (#2) that emphasized *burial* and another (#3) that repeatedly introduced the *crowd*. And now, in unexpected fashion, onto the stage come

proached Philip, who was from Bethsaida in Galilee, and put this request to
him: "Sir, we should like to see Jesus."
[22]Philip went to tell Andrew; Philip and
Andrew in turn came to inform Jesus.
[23]Jesus answered them:

"The hour has come
for the Son of Man to be glorified.

24 I solemnly assure you,
unless the grain of wheat falls to the
earth and dies,
it remains just a grain of wheat.
But if it dies,
it produces much fruit.

25 The man who loves his life
loses it,
while the man who hates his life in
this world
preserves it to life eternal.

26 If anyone would serve me,

let him follow me;
where I am,
there will my servant be.
If anyone serves me,
him the Father will honor.

27 My soul is troubled now,
yet what should I say—
Father, save me from this hour?
But it was for this that I came to this
hour.

28 Father, glorify your name!"

Then a voice came from the sky:

"I have glorified it,
and will glorify it again."

[29]When the crowd of bystanders heard
the voice, they said it was thunder.
Others maintained, "An angel was
speaking to him." [30]Jesus answered,
"That voice did not come for my sake,
but for yours.

"some Greeks" (v. 20), who start a move toward Jesus through the aid of our
typical missionaries (1:41, 45; 6:5-10), Philip and Andrew. Those following
Jesus now include both Jews and Greeks, the latter peculiarly illustrative of
"the whole world running after him" (v. 19).

In the verses that follow, John begins to pull the whole chapter
together—the burial ointment, the great crowd, the Greeks, the whole
world. The narratives will now be interpreted by Jesus' words. The HOUR
has come (v. 23) in which Jesus will be glorified, that is, in which God will
manifest to the utmost his presence in his Son. But this hour entails death:
the grain of wheat must fall into the ground if it is to produce fruit (v. 24).
Jesus will enter the ground (the burial ointment of verse 7 is an advance
statement of that), and his dying will produce much fruit. We have begun to
see the whole world going after him—the Jewish crowds of verses 9, 12, 17,
18, 29, 34 as well as the first fruits of the Gentile harvest (vv. 20-22). It is
this same teaching, but in different words, that Jesus proclaims in verse 32:
". . . and I—once I am lifted up from earth—will draw all men to myself."
The beginning of this being lifted up will be Jesus' crucifixion.

What Jesus is insisting upon in this episode is that life will be offered to
the world *through* his death. If he is buried like the seed, if he is lifted onto
the cross, then much fruit will come; then he will draw all to himself. The
crowd and the Greeks are simply the initial harvest. And, in a remarkable
way, this being buried, this being raised on a cross, is also Jesus' glorification (vv. 23, 28), the manifestation in him of his Father's presence, nowhere

31 "Now has judgment come upon this
world,
now will this world's prince be
driven out,
32 and I—once I am lifted up from
earth—
will draw all men to myself."

33(This statement indicated the sort of
death he had to die.) 34The crowd objected to his words: "We have heard it
said in the law that the Messiah is to remain forever. How can you claim that
the Son of Man must be lifted up? Just
who is this 'Son of Man'?" 35Jesus answered:
"The light is among you only a little
longer.

Walk while you still have it
or darkness will come over you.
The man who walks in the dark
does not know where he is going.
36 While you have the light,
keep faith in the light;
thus you will become sons of light."

After this utterance, Jesus left them and
went into hiding.

Evaluation of the Ministry. 37Despite
his many signs performed in their presence, they refused to believe in him.
38This was to fulfill the word of the
prophet Isaiah:
"Lord, who has believed what has
reached our ears?

more evident than in Jesus' act of self-sacrificing love. (So, too, does Isaiah's
servant song join to the death of the servant his glorification and elevation.
John's theology flows from Isa 52:13: "See, my servant shall prosper, he
shall be *raised high* and greatly *exalted* [glorified].")

As Jesus mentions his own self-giving (vv. 23-24), he joins to it that of
his disciples. They are called to identical servant roles (vv. 25-26).

Verses 27-30 are strangely reminiscent of the agony in the garden—
missing in the Fourth Gospel, for which it may present a too human Jesus.
Yet at this point, as in the garden scene, Jesus' soul is troubled, and he is
tempted to pray for the hour's passing—yet he doesn't (v. 37). Rather, reinforcement comes from the Father, who has glorified (manifested) himself
through the signs and will glorify himself even further through Jesus' resurrection (v. 38). Lines are being drawn, since the manifestation of God's loving presence at the moment of crucifixion will demand reaction, and the
reaction will determine individual judgment (v. 37). The world's prince of
darkness will be driven out by the light that is Jesus. The present moment,
however, is the hour of Jesus' sunset. "The light is among you only a little
longer. Walk while you still have it . . . . " (v. 35). As Jesus leaves the scene
(v. 36) and the ministry of the signs ends, some are still stumbling in the
darkness: "How can you claim that the Son of Man must be lifted up? Just
who is this Son of Man?" (v. 34).

5. The evangelist's evaluation (12:37-43). The signs' ministry has been
no great success, neither in Jesus' lifetime nor in the later preaching of them
by Jesus' disciples. It is as though Isa 53:1 had been written for this occasion:
"Lord, who has believed what has reached our ears?" Paul would have the

To whom has the might of the Lord been revealed?"

³⁹The reason they could not believe was that, as Isaiah says elsewhere:

⁴⁰ "He has blinded their eyes,
and numbed their hearts,
lest they see
or comprehend,
or have a change of heart—
and I should heal them."

⁴¹Isaiah uttered these words because he had seen Jesus' glory, and it was of him he spoke.

⁴²There were many, even among the Sanhedrin, who believed in him; but they refused to admit it because of the Pharisees, for fear they might be ejected from the synagogue. ⁴³They preferred the praise of men to the glory of God.

Summary Proclamation

⁴⁴Jesus proclaimed aloud:
"Whoever puts faith in me
believes not so much in me
as in him who sent me;
⁴⁵ and whoever looks on me
is seeing him who sent me.
⁴⁶ I have come to the world as its light,
to keep anyone who believes in me
from remaining in the dark.
⁴⁷ If anyone hears my words and does

same feeling with regard to his own preaching ministry (Rom 10:16). It is as though Isa 6:10, too, had been written for Jesus' times. The sad comment of verse 40 was well known and often used in the early church (Mark 4:12; Matt 13:15; Luke 8:10; Rom 11:8; Acts 28:26). It is not a proclamation of predestination. Any blinding and hardening that occur are always seen as a penance that follows personal guilt. Isaiah's text was meant to inform the prophet—and numerous preachers after him—that the comparative failure of his mission entered somehow into God's plan and should not discourage him.

Verse 41 could be clearer for us poor readers in the twentieth century. In what way did Isaiah, living centuries before Jesus, see his glory? This must refer back to the contexts of the quotes from Isa 53 and 6. In the first, Isaiah speaks of the servant; in the second, of his inaugural glorious vision of God as King and Lord of hosts. In God's glory, he has seen that of Jesus, for the Father shares it with him; and it is with the same glory that the servant has been exalted.

Verses 42-43 introduce us to a fringe group of disciples, crypto-Christians, who hid their feeble faith in Jesus lest, like the man born blind in chapter 9, they be expelled from the synagogue. John is writing now about such Christians of his own generation.

6. Jesus' summary proclamation (12:44-50). There is no attempt here to indicate an occasion or audience for these verses. What we have, rather, is a résumé of the salient points of Jesus' teaching, in his own words, located here by John as a recapitulation before starting the account of Jesus' passion-glorification. Reappearing in summary fashion is the statement of (a) the union of Father and Son (vv. 44-45); (b) Jesus as light of the world,

not keep them,
I am not the one to condemn him,
for I did not come to condemn the
world
but to save it.
48 Whoever rejects me and does not
accept my words
already has his judge,
namely, the word I have spoken—
it is that which will condemn him
on the last day.
49 For I have not spoken on my own;

no, the Father who sent me
has commanded me
what to say and how to speak.
50 Since I know that his commandment means eternal life,
whatever I say
is spoken just as he instructed me."

III. THE BOOK OF GLORY

13 The Washing of the Feet. ¹Before
the feast of Passover, Jesus realized that the hour had come for him to

come not to condemn but to save (vv. 46-47); (c) the inevitable judgment
that depends on personal reaction (v. 48); (d) the identification of Jesus'
word with that of the Father and of the eternal life that it gives (vv. 49-50).
These themes have been constantly cycled through these first twelve
chapters.

As we come to the conclusion of this first half of John's Gospel, it might
be of help to review very briefly what the sign theology has involved. By
means of signs—seven of them are miracles—the evangelist has attempted
to tell us who Jesus is and what he has effected, so that by knowing Jesus we
might know the Father. The seven miracle-signs have taught us that the new
era of messianic wine has arrived (Cana); that Jesus' word is life-giving (the
official's son, the infirm man at the pool); that Jesus is the bread of life and
the saving presence of God (ch. 6); and that he is, finally, both the light (ch.
9) and the life (ch. 11) of the world. If this is who Jesus is and what Jesus
does, it is perforce who God is and what God does; for Jesus, by word and
action, reveals the Father. Thus far can the signs take us. But if we really
want to advance from this position to know Jesus and the Father in the very
heart of their being, we must take a further step. Jesus' passion will reveal
both him and his Father in their heart of hearts.

C. THE BOOK OF GLORY

John 13:1–20:31

With chapter 13, we turn from Jesus' public ministry and its revelatory
signs to Jesus' last days, to the period of his glorification, that is, his death
and resurrection, in which God's glory, God's presence, will be manifested.
For this reason, this second half of the Gospel is frequently entitled "The
Book of Glory." It includes the farewell discourses (chs. 13–17), the passion
narrative (chs. 18–19), the resurrection (ch. 20), and the epilogue (ch. 21).

pass from this world to the Father. He had loved his own in this world, and would show his love for them to the end. ²The devil had already induced Judas, son of Simon Iscariot, to hand him over; and so, during the supper, ³Jesus—fully aware that he had come from God and was going to God, the Father who had handed everything over to him—⁴rose from the meal and took off his cloak. He picked up a towel and tied it around himself. ⁵Then he poured water into a basin and began to wash his disciples' feet and dry them with the towel he had around him. ⁶Thus he came to Simon Peter, who said to him, "Lord, are you going to wash my feet?" ⁷Jesus answered, "You may not realize now what I am doing, but later you will understand." ⁸Peter replied, "You shall never wash my feet!" "If I do not wash you," Jesus answered, "you will have no share in my heritage." ⁹"Lord," Simon Peter said to him, "then not only my feet, but my hands and head as well." ¹⁰Jesus told him, "The man who has bathed has no need to wash [except for his feet]; he is entirely cleansed, just as

13:1–17:26 The Farewell Discourses

These five chapters veer sharply from the previous presentation of Jesus' ministerial signs to an insistence on the Christian's actual, realized life in Jesus. The emphasis is not on the future but on the present. We hear the voice of Jesus, as though already risen and glorified, speaking to his disciples of present life, of indwelling, of love, of effected judgment, of the Spirit Paraclete who is at once both advocate and revealer. Jesus leaves to go to the Father and, in a little while, to return. The central stress is on union: the union of Father and Son; the gift and indwelling presence of their Spirit; the union of Son and disciples; the union of disciples with one another. The dynamism of all this is *love*, a word that now begins to take over John's good news. If we really want to know who and what Jesus is, so that we might know who and what God is, LOVE is the answer.

1. The opening scene: foot-washing (13:1-30). Again we approach Passover season (v. 1). But this time it will be Jesus' own passover from this world to the Father (vv. 1, 3). In this dramatic scene, Jesus, servant of the Father, becomes the servant of humankind. His hour has come, and he loves his friends "to the end" (v. 1), a Johannine double-entendre that includes both time and measure. Jesus does the servant task (cf. Luke 22:27); so, too, must his disciples serve one another. We are all called to wash one another's feet. All this is clear, and it is enunciated precisely by Jesus to remove any possible doubt (vv. 12-17).

Verses 6-10, however, are confusing. They seem to have a different thrust. What Jesus does cannot be understood till later (v. 7). Peter objects, as he did to Jesus' servant *death* in Mark 8:32; the washing, or rather, the being washed, is so important that without it the disciples can have no part in Jesus (v. 8). This reads like more than a simple example of Christian service and has tempted many commentators to believe that this *servant foot-*

you are; though not all." [11](The reason he said, "Not all are washed clean," was that he knew his betrayer.)

[12]After he had washed their feet, he put his cloak back on and reclined at table once more. He said to them:

"Do you understand what I just did for you?
[13] You address me as 'Teacher' and 'Lord,'
and fittingly enough,
for that is what I am.
[14] But if I washed your feet —
I who am Teacher and Lord —
then you must wash each other's feet.
[15] What I just did was to give you an example:
as I have done, so you must do.
[16] I solemnly assure you,

no slave is greater than his master;
no messenger outranks the one who sent him.
[17] Once you know all these things,
blest will you be if you put them into practice.

Role of Judas

[18] "What I say is not said of all,
for I know the kind of men I chose.
My purpose here is the fulfillment of Scripture:
'He who partook of bread with me has raised his heel against me.'
[19] I tell you this now, before it takes place,
so that when it takes place you may believe
that I AM.
[20] I solemnly assure you,

washing is also symbolic of Jesus' *servant death*. Moreover, the absolutely essential washing of verse 8 is reminiscent of baptismal teaching.

These clues suggest that the theology here is particularly rich, even though obscure. (a) Jesus' servant foot-washing is symbolic of his servant death. (b) Participation in this salvific death is through baptism, without which "you will have no share in my heritage" (v. 8) and through which we are "entirely cleansed" and need not be washed again (v. 10). The line runs from symbolized salvific death to sacramental participation. (c) All this, in turn, leads to the ethical servant role that we must live with regard to one another (vv. 12-17). Baptized into Jesus' salvific death, we must lead his servant life. "What I just did was to give you an example: as I have done, so you must do" (v. 15). This is a prophetic-action description of the role of all Christians, but especially of authority (like Peter) in the church. This must be exercised on one's knees before the people of God. Peter's difficulty with Christ's servant role — a difficulty felt a million times over by church authorities and ordinary Christians down through the centuries — reminds us of his similar difficulty in Mark 8:32-33.

One disciple is not clean. At this "hour," at this initiation of final conflict, he denies his share with Jesus, he refuses belief in the I AM (v. 19). He too passes over, but into the power of Satan (vv. 2, 27). Judas Iscariot, table companion of the Lord (v. 18, citing Ps 41:9), will now desert the light of the world. As he passes from light to darkness, the evangelist notes significantly and sadly, "It was night" (v. 30).

he who accepts anyone I send
accepts me,
and in accepting me
accepts him who sent me."
²¹After saying this, Jesus grew deeply
troubled. He went on to give this testimony:

"I tell you solemnly,
one of you will betray me."
²²The disciples looked at one another,
puzzled as to whom he could mean.
²³One of them, the disciple whom Jesus
loved, reclined close to him as they ate.
²⁴Simon Peter signaled him to ask Jesus
whom he meant. ²⁵He leaned back
against Jesus' chest and said to him,
"Lord, who is he?" ²⁶Jesus answered,
"The one to whom I give the bit of food I
dip in the dish." He dipped the morsel,
then took it and gave it to Judas, son of
Simon Iscariot. ²⁷Immediately after,

Satan entered his heart. Jesus addressed
himself to him, "Be quick about what
you are to do." ²⁸(Naturally, none of
those reclining at table understood why
Jesus said this to him. ²⁹A few had the
idea that, since Judas held the common
purse, Jesus was telling him to buy what
was needed for the feast, or to give
something to the poor.) ³⁰No sooner had
Judas eaten the morsel than he went out.
It was night.

³¹Once Judas had left, Jesus said:
"Now is the Son of Man glorified
and God is glorified in him.
32 [If God has been glorified in him,]
God will, in turn, glorify him in
himself,
and will glorify him soon.
33 My children, I am not to be with
you much longer.
You will look for me,

This insistence on Judas underlines a problem felt by the first Christians
and, perhaps, tossed up at them in controversies. What did Judas' act of
betrayal say about Jesus' wisdom and knowledge? Could the true Messiah
have made so unfitting and fatal a choice? These questions were felt so
strongly in the early church that Judas receives special attention in all four
Gospels, as well as in Acts 1:15-26. John insists that Jesus knew of the
betrayal and that it fit into God's saving plan.

Verse 23 speaks for the first time of "the disciple whom Jesus loved." No
name is given, but his function is significant. Close to Jesus' side — as was the
Word to the Father's side in 1:18 — he mediates between Jesus and Peter; his
subsequent appearances will almost invariably be related to Peter.

2. Jesus' departure and return (13:31–14:31). Once Judas has left the
light, Jesus begins to speak to his own, his dearest friends. Various disciples
— Peter, Thomas, Philip, Judas — carry the discussion forward by the questions they pose. This enables us to break down the whole, hopefully to see it
more clearly, by dividing it according to the characters who ask the leading
questions.

a) The first section (13:31-35) is simply an introduction. Judas' departure
has set in motion the events of the passion. Jesus will be glorified, God will
be glorified, since God's presence as infinite love is about to be manifested in
Jesus. Jesus will leave, and that absence (or is it presence?) is the problem
underlying this whole section. As he leaves, he leaves behind his one essen-

but I say to you now
what I once said to the Jews:
'Where I am going, you cannot
come.'
34 I give you a new commandment:
Love one another.
Such as my love has been for you,
so must your love be for each other.
35 This is how all will know you for
my disciples:
your love for one another."
Peter's Denial Predicted. ³⁶"Lord,"
Simon Peter said to him, "where do you
mean to go?" Jesus answered:

"I am going where you cannot
follow me now;
later on you shall come after me."

³⁷"Lord," Peter said to him, "why can I
not follow you now? I will lay down my

life for you!" ³⁸"You will lay down your
life for me, will you?" Jesus answered. "I
tell you truly, the cock will not crow
before you have three times disowned
me!

Last Discourse

14 ¹"Do not let your hearts be
troubled.
Have faith in God
and faith in me.
2 In my Father's house there are many
dwelling places;
otherwise, how could I have told
you
that I was going to prepare a place
for you?
3 I am indeed going to prepare a place
for you,
and then I shall come back to take

tial commandment: "Love one another" (v. 34). It is a *new* commandment because this mutual love must be modeled on something new — on the love that Jesus shows for his disciples. Mutual love must be the sign, the indispensable sign, of their discipleship.

b) *Peter* (13:36–14:4) moves the discussion further: "Lord, where do you mean to go?" (13:36). This appearance of Peter permits the evangelist to present a bit of tradition shared, seemingly, by the whole church, that Jesus predicted Peter's denial (13:37-38). Yet, though Peter would deny his Lord, he would also follow him in death (v. 36).

In the subsequent verses (14:1-4), the basic problems that control the rest of the chapter are touched upon. The disciples are troubled (v. 1, as also v. 27) — and so later will be John's own community — because of Jesus' departure. In response, Jesus insists on the necessity of faith, stating that he goes to prepare a place for them and will return to take them with him (v. 3). This sounds very much like a promise of Jesus' future return as visible Lord of the world (the technical term for this is the *parousia* = coming). The early church awaited this with fervent hope (1 Thess 4:16-18). But John's Gospel will now reinterpret such a futuristic approach. Jesus has not passed over a bridge that was subsequently blown up; there is a *way* to him, and they already know it (v. 4).

c) So *Thomas* (14:5-7) asks, "How can we know the way?" Jesus' answer states that Christian hope is not in a method, not in a procedure, but in a person. Jesus himself is "the way, and the truth, and the life" (v. 6). Through and in Jesus, one *comes to* the Father, *knows* the Father, *sees* the Father.

you with me,
that where I am you also may be.
4 You know the way that leads where
I go."
⁵"Lord," said Thomas, "we do not know
where you are going. How can we know
the way?" ⁶Jesus told him:
"I am the way, and the truth, and
the life;
no one comes to the Father but
through me.
7 If you really knew me, you would
know my Father also.
From this point on you know him;
you have seen him."
⁸"Lord," Philip said to him, "show us
the Father and that will be enough for
us." ⁹"Philip," Jesus replied, "after I have

been with you all this time, you still do
not know me?
"Whoever has seen me has seen the
Father.
How can you say, 'Show us the Father'?
10 Do you not believe that I am in
the Father
and the Father is in me?
The words I speak are not spoken
of myself;
it is the Father who lives in me
accomplishing his works.
11 Believe me that I am in the Father
and the Father is in me,
or else, believe because of the works
I do.
12 I solemnly assure you,

d) *Philip* (14:8-21) seizes on that final phrase to ask: "Lord, show us the Father . . . ." (v. 8). One can hear the sigh of weariness, almost of failure, in Jesus' voice: "Philip, after I have been with you all this time, you still do not know me? Whoever has seen me has seen the Father" (v. 9). And the discussion continues, pointing to the perfect union of Jesus with the Father: both his words and his works are the Father's (vv. 10-11). With this, Jesus turns his attention to the disciples. They, too, will do the works that Jesus has done because he will respond according to their petitions, so that God will be manifested in the Son. The disciples' love will bring from the Father another Paraclete, the Spirit of truth, to remain with them always (v. 16). In this sense, Jesus will come back; they will not be left orphans (v. 18).

At this point, the reader's head should be spinning a bit. What is going on? What seemed to be a statement of Jesus' future return to take his disciples to places prepared for them (14:3), a movement carrying believers into some future and unknown paradise, has subtly turned around like a boomerang targeting in on the place from which it was originally launched. Jesus goes, but he returns; and the dwelling places he prepares, which seemed to be located out there somewhere (v. 2), will be found, rather, within the believers themselves (vv. 20-21). In some way, this return is connected with another Paraclete (cf. 1 John 2:1, where Jesus is called the first one) who takes Jesus' place as both advocate and revealer.

It is this boomerang movement — Jesus' departure and consequent return through the Paraclete — that explains the "little while" in verse 19. Just as the disciples see Jesus now, so they will soon know of his union with the Father,

the man who has faith in me
will do the works I do,
and greater far than these.
Why? Because I go to the Father,

13 and whatever you ask in my name
I will do,
so as to glorify the Father in the
Son.

14 Anything you ask me in my name
I will do.

15 If you love me
and obey the commands I give you.

16 I will ask the Father
and he will give you another Paraclete —
to be with you always:

17 the Spirit of truth,
whom the world cannot accept,
since it neither sees him nor recognizes him;
but you can recognize him
because he remains with you
and will be within you.

18 I will not leave you orphaned;
I will come back to you.

19 A little while now and the world
will see me no more;
but you see me

as one who has life, and you will
have life.

20 On that day you will know
that I am in my Father,
and you in me, and I in you.

21 He who obeys the commandments
he has from me
is the man who loves me;
and he who loves me will be loved
by my Father.
I too will love him
and reveal myself to him."

22Judas (not Judas Iscariot) said to him,
"Lord, why is it that you will reveal
yourself to us and not to the world?"

23Jesus answered:

"Anyone who loves me
will be true to my word,
and my Father will love him;
we will come to him
and make our dwelling place with
him.

24 He who does not love me does not
keep my words.
Yet the word you hear is not mine;
it comes from the Father who sent
me.

which union he will share with them. The disciples who love will be loved by both the Father and Son, who (through the Paraclete?) will reveal himself to them (v. 21). All they could have hoped for in the future will soon be now.

e) This provokes the *Judas* (not Iscariot) sequence (14:22-31). How strange that Jesus should speak of all this Spirit return, indwelling, union with Father and disciples, when what Judas and the others were expecting was a visible return in majesty accompanied by a fearsome display of celestial fireworks. "Lord, why is it that you will reveal yourself to us and not to the world?" (v. 22). Jesus' answer almost avoids the question as it merely insists on what has already been proclaimed. He and the Father will come to those who love and will dwell with them (vv. 23-24). (This, for John, is the all-important coming, *parousia*, of the Lord.) This coming is directly related to the Paraclete whom the Father will send to instruct and to remind. John's community is clearly a Paraclete community, confident that the Spirit, Jesus' Spirit, is with them still, reminding them of, and interpreting, Jesus'

25 This much have I told you while I
was still with you;
26 the Paraclete, the Holy Spirit
whom the Father will send in my
name,
will instruct you in everything,
and remind you of all that I told
you.
27 'Peace' is my farewell to you,
my peace is my gift to you;
I do not give it to you as the world
gives peace.
Do not be distressed or fearful.
28 You have heard me say,
'I go away for a while, and I come
back to you.'
If you truly loved me
you would rejoice to have me go to
the Father,
for the Father is greater than I.
29 I tell you this now, before it takes
place,
so that when it takes place you may
believe.
30 I shall not go on speaking to you
longer;
the Prince of this world is at hand.

He has no hold on me,
31 but the world must know that I
love the Father
and do as the Father has commanded me.
Come, then! Let us be on our way.

The Vine and the Branches

15 1"I am the true vine
and my Father is the vine-
grower.
2 He prunes away
every barren branch,
but the fruitful ones
he trims clean
to increase their yield.
3 You are clean already,
thanks to the word I have spoken
to you.
4 Live on in me, as I do in you.
No more than a branch can bear
fruit of itself
apart from the vine,
can you bear fruit
apart from me.
5 I am the vine, you are the branches.
He who lives in me and I in him,

words, instructing them with the words and wisdom of the Lord. Surely this Gospel is filled with Paraclete reminders and instruction.

The fear and distress of people awaiting a delayed future return (vv. 1, 27) must give way in John's community to the peace that is Christ's gift, to the joy that is theirs at the knowledge that Jesus has returned to the Father who is his origin, "greater than I" (v. 28).

This discussion, says Jesus, is long enough; now it is time to face the conflict with the Prince of this world (v. 30). The Father has commanded total love, and the world will soon know that this is what the Son will give. "Come, then! Let us be on our way" (v. 31).

3. Discourse on Jesus and his community (15:1–16:33). There are two major difficulties with this material. The *first* is that it is completely unexpected. Seemingly 14:31 has just set Jesus and his disciples in motion: "Let us be on our way." What would follow naturally after this is 18:1, "After this discourse, Jesus went out with his disciples across the Kidron Valley." But between 14:31 and 18:1 we have all the material, almost all discourse, of chapters 15–17.

will produce abundantly,
for apart from me you can do
nothing.

6 A man who does not live in me
is like a withered, rejected branch,
picked up to be thrown in the fire
and burnt.

7 If you live in me,
and my words stay part of you
you may ask what you will —
it will be done for you.

8 My Father has been glorified
in your bearing much fruit
and becoming my disciples.

A Disciple's Love

9 "As the Father has loved me,
so I have loved you.
Live on in my love.

10 You will live in my love
if you keep my commandments,
even as I have kept my Father's
commandments,
and live in his love.

11 All this I tell you
that my joy may be yours
and your joy may be complete.

12 This is my commandment:
love one another
as I have loved you.

13 There is no greater love than this:
to lay down one's life for one's
friends.

14 You are my friends
if you do what I command you.

15 I no longer speak of you as slaves,
for a slave does not know what his
master is about.

A *second* difficulty is that chapters 15–16 repeat much of what has already been said in chapter 14. Jesus talks again of indwelling, of the Paraclete, of departure and return, of love, of the "little while." These facts have led numerous students of John to detect here an addition, some kind of parallel to, or alternative version of, chapter 14. This is highly probable. Yet, if chapters 15–16 are an addition, they are surely not an intrusion; they are not a detour, but a circling around the same center. The motifs of chapter 14 appear, disappear, reappear. Not new knowledge, but reinforcement of the already given, seems to be the purpose of these two chapters. They divide themselves into one long monologue, followed by a combination of dialogue plus monologue.

a) *The long monologue* (15:1–16:16)

This is the longest monologue in the Fourth Gospel. It begins with:

i) The allegory of the vine (15:1–17)

The ancient Old Testament allegory of Israel as Yahweh's vine (Ps 80:9-20 is one example among many) becomes deeply Christianized at this point. Jesus is the true vine (vv. 1, 5) of which the Father takes personal care, pruning the barren branches, trimming clean the fruitful. These latter are the disciples who have accepted Jesus' life-giving word (vv. 3, 7). They are invited, encouraged to live on, to abide in Jesus. (The Greek word for "abide," *menō*, occurs eleven times in these few verses, a repeated insistence on the return of Jesus by indwelling. It is, however, translated in various

Instead, I call you friends,
since I have made known to you all
that I heard from my Father.

16 It was not you who chose me,
it was I who chose you
to go forth and bear fruit.
Your fruit must endure,
so that all you ask the Father in my name
he will give you.

17 The command I give you is this,
that you love one another.

The World's Hate

18 "If you find that the world hates you,
know it has hated me before you.

19 If you belonged to the world,
it would love you as its own;
the reason it hates you
is that you do not belong to the world.
But I chose you out of the world.

20 Remember what I told you:
no slave is greater than his master.

ways in our English text.) The other all-important word here is "love." Just as "live on," "stay part of," synonyms for the repeated "abide" are the essential phrases of verses 1-8, so "love" becomes essential in verses 9-17, while both bring this minor section to its conclusion in the "endure" and "love one another" of verses 16-17. The central teaching of this allegory is clear. *Abiding in Jesus through love* is what this little homily is all about. If this happens, when it happens, the disciple will produce fruit (vv. 5, 8). When it does not happen, the disciple is no disciple at all but "a withered, rejected branch" (v. 6), good for nothing but fuel.

The love of which Jesus speaks is one, but many. It begins with the Father's love for Christ (v. 9), moves on to Jesus' love for his friends (vv. 9, 12-13), is reciprocated in the disciples' loving obedience to Christ (vv. 10, 14), and radiates out through their love for one another (vv. 12, 17). It is this love that will be the source of their joy (v. 11) and the essential condition of their intimate friendship with the Lord (vv. 14-15). The model of love for all true discipleship is extreme, limitless; for it is Jesus himself who lays down his life for his friends (v. 13), as does the good shepherd of 10:11, 15, 17, 18. Yet it is precisely for love like this that Jesus has chosen them. They will bring forth enduring fruit, their prayers will be answered, to the extent that they love one another (vv. 16-17).

ii) Hatred from a hostile world (15:18–16:4a)

The words of the text are clear, as is the logical progression. The disciples are warned that the price of discipleship will be high. Just as Jesus was hated, as he was persecuted ("harried," v. 20), as his words were not accepted, so will it be for his followers — hated, persecuted, unaccepted by the world (vv. 18-20). Such will be the *fact*, a fact seemingly well known in the experience of John's community. The deep-down *crime* is that the adversaries have seen the evidence yet refuse to believe. Jesus has spoken to them (v. 22), he has performed works never done before (v. 24); yet they really

They will harry you
as they harried me.
They will respect your words
as much as they respected mine.
21 All this they will do to you because
of my name,
for they know nothing of him who
sent me.
22 If I had not come to them and
spoken to them,
they would not be guilty of sin;
now, however, their sin cannot be
excused.
23 To hate me is to hate my Father.
24 Had I not performed such works
among them
as no one has ever done before,
they would not be guilty of sin;
but as it is, they have seen,
and they go on hating me and my
Father.
25 However, this only fulfills the text
in their law:
'They hated me without cause.'
26 When the Paraclete comes,
the Spirit of truth who comes from
the Father —
and whom I myself will send from
the Father —
he will bear witness on my behalf.
27 You must bear witness as well,
for you have been with me from the
beginning.

16 ¹"I have told you all this
to keep your faith from being
shaken.
2 Not only will they expel you from
synagogues;
a time will come
when anyone who puts you to
death
will claim to be serving God!
3 All this they will do [to you]
because they knew neither the

know nothing about the Father who sent Jesus (v. 21), and in hating him, they hate the Father also (vv. 23-24). In the words of Ps 69:4, "They hated me without cause." *Witnesses* to the crime will be both the Paraclete and the disciples, who, having seen from the beginning, can bear witness to all (vv. 26-27). The *reason* why this subject comes up at all is that excommunication and even death await the disciples (16:2-3). May their faith not be shattered in such periods of terror (16:1, 4)!

Our text here has been paraphrased easily. Two issues, however, need explanation. The *first* is Jesus' use of the word "world" (vv. 18-19). In the present context, "world" has a strong negative content, quite different certainly from its beautiful appearance in chapter 3: "God so loved the world that he gave his only Son, that whoever believes in him may not die but may have eternal life. God did not send the Son into the world to condemn the world, but that the world might be saved through him" (3:16-17). This world that God loves with infinite love, that he saves and does not condemn, seems oceans apart from the hating and persecuting world of chapters 15–16. One identical word is being used in completely different fashions. This is a difficulty in John's Gospel that we must keep before our eyes. The "world" can be the work of God's hands (1:2-4), the object of his love (3:16-17) — that is God's world. But there is another world, too, what we in the twentieth century might call the epitome of worldliness, in which

Father nor me.

4 But I have told you these things
that when their hour comes
you may remember my telling you
of them.

Jesus' Departure; Coming of the Paraclete

"I did not speak of this with you
from the beginning
because I was with you.

5 Now that I go back to him who
sent me,
not one of you asks me, 'Where are
you going?'

6 Because I have had all this to say
to you,
you are overcome with grief.

7 Yet I tell you the sober truth:
It is much better for you that I go.
If I fail to go,
the Paraclete will never come to
you,
whereas if I go,
I will send him to you.

8 When he comes,
he will prove the world wrong
about sin,
about justice,
about condemnation.

9 About sin—
in that they refuse to believe in me;

10 about justice—
from the fact that I go to the Father
and you can see me no more;

11 about condemnation—

reign darkness and hatred, untruth and death. Of this world, better entitled "anti-world," Satan is prince (14:30; 16:11). John's community has already encountered it.

This brings us to the *second* issue. We find once more a historical bi-level. Expulsion from the synagogue (9:22; 12:42), even death, has touched the Johannine Christians; and this they see as the lot of those who follow the Master (15:18-21). Seemingly, persecution and disbelief have widened in their experience, being found not only in non-Christian Judaism but also among the Gentiles. In this sense, a whole segment of God's world has been transformed for them into a force of disbelief and hatred.

iii) The Paraclete (16:4b-16)

The Paraclete was barely mentioned in the final verses of chapter 15, but will now be the center of discussion. Jesus' departure, followed by persecution, was not a necessary subject of discourse at the beginning of the ministry, since it was not yet imminent (v. 4b). Not surprisingly, to speak of it now brings grief to the disciples. (To record that no one asks, "Where are you going?" [v. 5] ignores that very question raised by Peter in 13:36 and alluded to by Thomas in 14:5, an indication that chapter 16 is of different origin.) Jesus insists that grief is improper, for only his departure will assure the coming of the Paraclete. Into the Jesus-vacuum will come the Paraclete-presence. This divine presence, effectively experienced by John's community, will be proof positive that disbelief was sin, that justice was accomplished through Jesus' passage to the Father, that the prince of evil has been condemned to defeat (vv. 8-11).

for the prince of this world has been condemned.

12 I have much more to tell you,
but you cannot bear it now.

13 When he comes, however,
being the Spirit of truth
he will guide you to all truth.
He will not speak on his own,
but will speak only what he hears,
and will announce to you the things to come.

14 In doing this he will give glory to me,
because he will have received from me
what he will announce to you.

15 All that the Father has belongs to me.
That is why I said that what he will announce to you
he will have from me.

16 Within a short time you will lose sight of me,
but soon after that you shall see me again."

The Return of Jesus. [17]At this, some of his disciples asked one another: "What can he mean, 'Within a short time you will lose sight of me, but soon after that you will see me'? And did he not say that he is going back to the Father?" [18]They kept asking: "What does he mean by this 'short time'? We do not know what he is talking about." [19]Since Jesus was aware that they wanted to question him, he said: "You are asking one another about my saying, 'Within a short time you will lose sight of me, but soon after that you will see me.'

20 "I tell you truly:
you will weep and mourn
while the world rejoices;
you will grieve for a time,
but your grief will be turned to joy.

21 When a woman is in labor
she is sad that her time has come.
When she has borne her child,
she no longer remembers her pain
for joy that a man has been born

The Paraclete will do even more. As the Spirit of truth, he will be the constant guide of the disciples, speaking to them (through inspired preachers and writers like the evangelist) what he *hears* from Jesus, who, in turn, receives from the Father. The verbal form "he *hears*" (v. 13) is important. It places the Paraclete's function simultaneously in God's eternity and the reader's now. Through the Paraclete, what Jesus says in his Father's realm is *now* transmitted to the disciples. Jesus who once spoke in the flesh now speaks through the Spirit. Much of this present discourse, surely, comes from Jesus speaking through his Spirit to the community. In this sense, Jesus' earthly departure is a gain, for it enables the glorified Jesus to be present. The disciples will lose him in earthly form within a short time but will soon receive him back again in Spirit (v. 16).

b) *From dialogue into monologue into dialogue* (16:17-33)

The long monologue has ended, but there is still more to be recounted in a sort of dialogue between disciples and Master. Jesus' statement about the short time, the little while, brings the disciples back into view. What is meant by this "short time" (vv. 17-19)? Jesus does not answer the question directly but explains instead how grief will be turned into joy (see 20:20 for

into the world.

22 In the same way, you are sad for a
time,
but I shall see you again;
then your hearts will rejoice
with a joy no one can take from
you.

23 On that day you will have no questions to ask me.
I give you my assurance,
whatever you ask the Father,
he will give you in my name.

24 Until now you have not asked for
anything in my name.
Ask and you shall receive,
that your joy may be full.

25 I have spoken these things to you in
veiled language.
A time will come when I shall no
longer do so,
but shall tell you about the Father
in plain speech.

26 On that day you will ask in my
name
and I do not say that I will petition
the Father for you.

27 The Father already loves you,
because you have loved me
and have believed that I came from
God.

28 [I did indeed come from the Father;]
I came into the world.
Now I am leaving the world
to go to the Father."

29 "At last you are speaking plainly,"
his disciples exclaimed, "without talking
in veiled language! 30We are convinced
that you know everything. There is no
need for anyone to ask you questions.
We do indeed believe you came from
God." 31Jesus answered them:
"Do you really believe?

32 An hour is coming—has indeed already come—
when you will be scattered and
each will go his way,
leaving me quite alone.
(Yet I can never be alone;
the Father is with me.)

33 I tell you all this
that in me you may find peace.
You will suffer in the world.
But take courage!
I have overcome the world."

17 Completion of Jesus' Work.
¹After he had spoken these
words, Jesus looked up to heaven and
said:
"Father, the hour has come!

the actualization of this), like that of a mother once her child is born into the
world (vv. 20-22). On that day of birth, to continue the simile, the time of
veiled language will be over (vv. 23a, 25), and the time of direct and effective petition to the loving Father will have begun (vv. 23b-24, 26-27) for
those who have loved Jesus and believed in his divine origin (vv. 27-28).
When the disciples affirm their belief (v. 30b), Jesus gives a final warning.
During his hour they will be scattered, leaving him abandoned by all but his
Father (v. 32). They will suffer, yet only in Jesus is peace to be found. "Take
courage," he says to the disciples of then and now. The glorified Jesus has
already overcome the world (v. 33).

4. **Jesus' prayer (17:1-26).** These chapters of farewell discourse (chs.
13–17), with a precedent in the formal and final addresses of Moses (Deut
29–34), of Jacob (Gen 49), and of Paul (Acts 20:17-38), are brought to a fit-
ting conclusion by Jesus' prayer in chapter 17. This whole chapter is one

Give glory to your Son
that your Son may give glory to you,
2 inasmuch as you have given him authority over all mankind,
that he may bestow eternal life on those you gave him.
3 (Eternal life is this:
to know you, the only true God,
and him whom you have sent, Jesus Christ.)
4 I have given you glory on earth
by finishing the work you gave me to do.
5 Do you now, Father, give me glory at your side,
a glory I had with you before the world began.
6 I have made your name known
to those you gave me out of the world.
These men you gave me were yours;
they have kept your word.
7 Now they realize
that all that you gave me comes from you.
8 I entrusted to them
the message you entrusted to me,
and they received it.
They have known that in truth I came from you,
they have believed it was you who sent me.

long prayer directed by Jesus to the Father, his own solemn expansion, one might say, of the simple "Our Father" he taught his disciples in Matt 6 and Luke 11. Positioned between heaven and earth, between his Father and his disciples, Jesus prays for believers present and future. The prayer is often called Jesus' "Priestly Prayer." The title can be justified only if one believes that intercession is priestly, that the union for which Jesus prays is priestly work, that the consecration spoken of in verse 19 deals with sacrifice. Better, surely, to call it simply Christ's prayer for union.

a) *Division and content*

i) Father and Son (vv. 1-5)

In these five verses, Jesus speaks directly to his Father. The hour has come; the manifestation of the divine presence (glorification) is the task. Eternal life will consist in recognizing this divine presence. As the evangelist puts it in verse 3 — and this is his whole Logos, or word theology — "Eternal life is this: to know you, the only true God, and him whom you have sent, Jesus Christ." To know God in the Son whom he has sent is eternal life. Jesus has manifested that presence on earth (v. 4) and will now return to that presence at the Father's side (v. 5). He has finished the work given him to perform (v. 4). The true nature of God, which is love, is about to be manifested in Jesus' self-sacrificing death.

ii) Son and disciples (vv. 6-19)

Jesus' conversation with the Father now turns to the subject of the disciples. To them has Jesus made known the Father's name (presumably the I AM that the Father has shared with the Son), and they have accepted the

Prayer for the Disciples

9 "For these I pray —
not for the world
but for these you have given me,
for they are really yours.
10 (Just as all that belongs to me is
yours,
so all that belongs to you is mine.)
It is in them that I have been glorified.
11 I am in the world no more,
but these are in the world
as I come to you.

O Father most holy,
protect them with your name which
you have given me
[that they may be one, even as we
are one].
12 As long as I was with them,
I guarded them with your name
which you gave me.
I kept careful watch,
and not one of them was lost,
none but him who was destined to
be lost —
in fulfillment of Scripture.

13 Now, however, I come to you;
I say all this while I am still in the
world
that they may share my joy completely.
14 I gave them your word,
and the world has hated them for it;
they do not belong to the world
[any more than I belong to the
world].
15 I do not ask you to take them out
of the world,
but to guard them from the evil
one.
16 They are not of the world,
any more than I belong to the
world.
17 Consecrate them by means of
truth —
'Your word is truth.'
18 As you have sent me into the
world,
so I have sent them into the world;
19 I consecrate myself for their sakes
now,
that they may be consecrated in
truth.

word (v. 6) and the message (v. 8), believing that what Jesus has comes from him who sent him (vv. 7-8). In a word, they have believed in Jesus' divine origin and divine union.

It is for these disciples that Jesus prays at this moment of departure in verses 9-19. He prays specifically:

— "protect them with your name which you have given me" (v. 11);
— "that they may be one, even as we are one" (v. 11);
— "that they may share my joy completely" (v. 13);
— that the Father "guard them from the evil one" (v. 15);
— that he "consecrate them by means of truth" (v. 17).

In paraphrase, what Jesus asks for his disciples is that they be protected by the immense power of the I AM (which will be demonstrated graphically in 18:6); that their unity resemble, and be based on, the intimate union of Father and Son; that their sorrow be changed into the divine joy that the Son reflects from his Father; that they be guarded from the prince of this world; that they be truly consecrated — as is Jesus — in complete dedication to God's service, which will be a mission to the world (vv. 18-19).

Prayer for All Believers

20 "I do not pray for them alone.
   I pray also for those who will be-
      lieve in me through their word,
21 that all may be one
   as you, Father, are in me, and I in
      you;
   I pray that they may be [one] in us,

that the world may believe that you
   sent me.
22 I have given them the glory you
      gave me
   that they may be one, as we are
      one—
23 I living in them, you living in me—
   that their unity may be complete.

iii) Son and future disciples (vv. 20-26)

For future disciples, Jesus prays for one central gift—unity: "that all may
be one as you, Father, are in me and I in you . . . that they may be one in
us . . . that they may be one as we are one—I living in them, you living in
me—that their unity may be complete" (vv. 21-23). It will be only through
this evidence of loving unity that the mission to the world (v. 18) can be effective; for only if the loving union of disciples is apparent can the world
believe (v. 21), can the world know (v. 23) that the Father has sent Jesus and
that the Father's love can be found in the disciples as it can be found in Jesus
himself (v. 23). Where this loving unity of disciples is found, there too will
be found the company of Jesus (v. 24), the divine presence (v. 24), the
power of the divine name, and the living love of both Father and Son (v.
26).

b) *Recurring themes*

i) One cannot fail to note the frequent recurrence of "Father," a total of
six times (vv. 1, 5, 11, 21, 24, 25). This reflects Jesus' own unique use of the
Aramaic *Abba* ("loving Father"), with which he customarily began his
prayer. Perfectly joined to the Father in oneness, he remains at all times the
obedient and loving Son.

ii) The central motif of the prayer is that of unity—unity of present and
future disciples, a unity modeled on that of Father and Son, a union that
takes root from the love of Father and Son that is gifted to all disciples (v.
26).

iii) There is strong insistence on love: the Father's love for the disciples
(v. 23), the Father's love for Jesus (vv. 23-24), the Father's love for Jesus and
the disciples (v. 26). The Father's love is the supreme revelation of the
Gospel. Jesus, the incarnate Word, speaks the Father in one word—LOVE.
Throughout this whole prayer, it is clear that the church is meant to be a
community of love, the living sign or sacrament of the mutual love of
Father and Son.

So shall the world know that you
    sent me,
and that you loved them as you
    loved me.

24 Father,
all those you gave me
I would have in my company
where I am,
to see this glory of mine
which is your gift to me,
because of the love you bore me
    before the world began.

25 Just Father,

the world has not known you,
but I have known you;
and these men have known that
    you sent me.

26 To them I have revealed your
    name,
and I will continue to reveal it
so that your love for me may live
    in them,
and I may live in them."

18 **Jesus Arrested.** ¹After this discourse, Jesus went out with his disciples across the Kidron Valley. There

iv) The "world" is mentioned seventeen times in these verses. It is the world of anti-world, the center of disbelief and hatred and unlove, the contrast and contradiction to what Christian living should be. Judas (v. 12) is an example of one to whom all was offered and rejected, one who experienced light and life but left it for darkness and death. While this world is not here the object of Jesus' prayer, yet it is not a world for which Jesus has no hope or feeling. While the strong emphasis lies on prayer for Jesus' actual and future disciples, verses 21 and 23 do pray that, through Christian unity, the world may *believe* and *know* that Jesus has been sent by a loving Father.

c) *Echoes of the Our Father*

Though the customary "Our Father" is not found in the Fourth Gospel, there are tiny echoes of it that, fittingly enough, appear in this uniquely Johannine prayer. "Father," as we have seen, is found six times as Jesus' prayerful address. Reference to God's name—similar to "Hallowed be thy name"—occurs in verses 6, 11, 12, and 26. Reference to glorification in verses 1, 5, and 24 brings into view the divine presence, the hope of "Thy kingdom come." And the request (v. 15) that the disciples be guarded from the evil one echoes the similar and final request of the "Our Father" in Matt 6:13.

d) *Eucharistic material*

Concluding chapters 13–17, the reader must have noticed the lack of any mention of Eucharistic institution. Seemingly, the evangelist has chosen to locate his Eucharistic material at the end of chapter 6, where it brings the homily on the bread from heaven to a powerful conclusion. The vine allegory of chapter 15, however, may reveal an original Eucharistic setting, especially since its "live on in me" language parallels closely the "remains in me, and I in him" of 6:56.

was a garden there, and he and his disciples entered it. ²The place was familiar to Judas as well (the one who was to hand him over) because Jesus had often met there with his disciples. ³Judas took the cohort as well as guards supplied by the chief priests and the Pharisees, and came there with lanterns, torches and weapons. ⁴Jesus, aware of all that would happen to him, stepped forward and said to them, "Who is it you want?" ⁵"Jesus the Nazorean," they replied. "I am he," he answered. (Now Judas, the one who was to hand him over, was there with them.) ⁶As Jesus said to them, "I am he," they retreated slightly and fell to the ground. ⁷Jesus put the question to them again, "Who is it you want?" "Jesus the Nazorean," they repeated. ⁸"I have told you, I am he," Jesus said. "If I am the one you want, let these men go." ⁹(This was to fulfill what he had said, "I have not lost one of those you gave me.")

¹⁰Then Simon Peter, who had a sword, drew it and struck the slave of

18:1–19:42 The Passion Narrative

We now turn from discourses — at least four whole chapters worth — to narrative. Our feet come back to the ground after a head-and-heart trip through the world above where the Father and Son live in eternal unity and from which they will send the enlivening Paraclete. Here we find the earthly Jesus enroute to the passion and to that elevation on the cross that is the glorification of divine love. It is at this point in the Gospel that John presents material that, in both content and sequence, is quite similar to that of the other three Gospels.

1. The arrest (18:1-11). Jesus and his disciples exit through the city walls, moving eastward a short distance down and across the Kidron Valley to a garden. The name of the garden, Gethsemani, is not given (Mark 14:32; Matt 26:36), nor does John mention the agony found in the other Gospels. John's portrait of Jesus tends to omit characteristics that are, in his judgment, overly human. He must know of the agony, however, since echoes of it do appear, though with changed emphasis and context, in 12:27: "My soul is troubled now, yet what should I say — Father, save me from this hour?" and in 18:11: "Am I not to drink the cup the Father has given me?"

That "Jesus had often met there with his disciples" (v. 2) explains how Judas knows where to find him and agrees with the Johannine insistence on multiple visits to Jerusalem during Jesus' ministry. So it is here that Judas comes with forces from the Romans, "the cohort," and from the Jewish authorities (v. 3). The lanterns and torches provide a stage of light and darkness on which this dramatic scene will be played out. Jesus, armed with divine knowledge (v. 4), confronts his adversaries, including Judas (v. 5), the Satan figure of 6:70-71; 13:2, 27, with the question: "Who is it you want?" To their reply, "Jesus the Nazorean," Jesus answers with the majestic and awesome response, I AM — *egō eimi* (obscured, unfortunately, in our

81

the high priest, severing his right ear. (The slave's name was Malchus.) ¹¹At that Jesus said to Peter, "Put your sword back in its sheath. Am I not to drink the cup the Father has given me?"

¹²Then the soldiers of the cohort, their tribune, and the Jewish guards arrested Jesus and bound him. ¹³They led him first to Annas, the father-in-law of Caiaphas who was high priest that year. ¹⁴(It was Caiaphas who had proposed to the Jews the advantage of having one man die for the people.)

Peter's First Denial. ¹⁵Simon Peter, in company with another disciple, kept following Jesus closely. This disciple, who was known to the high priest, stayed with Jesus as far as the high priest's courtyard, ¹⁶while Peter was left standing at the gate. The disciple known to the high priest came out and spoke to the woman at the gate, and then brought Peter in. ¹⁷This servant girl who kept the gate said to Peter, "Are you not one of this man's followers?" "Not I," he replied.

¹⁸Now the night was cold, and the servants and the guards who were standing around had made a charcoal fire to warm themselves by. Peter joined them and stood there warming himself.

The Inquiry before Annas. ¹⁹The high priest questioned Jesus, first about his

translation, "I am he"). In the presence of the I AM, "they [Satan and his assistants] retreated slightly and fell to the ground" (v. 6) in compulsory adoration. Jesus, the one "sent" by the Father, is very much in control of his own destiny. He is in charge, also, of the destiny of his own sheep: "Let these men go" (v. 8). Jesus will not lose any of those whom his Father has given him (v. 9, and cf. 6:39; 10:28; 17:12).

The violent reaction of Peter's sword is paralleled in Mark 14:47, Matt 25:51, and Luke 22:50, though only John names Peter as the slasher and Malchus as the victim. (Oddly, both John and Luke agree that it was the *right* ear that was affected.) Jesus puts an immediate end to the violence. His food is to do his Father's will (4:34); his drink will be whatever the Father offers.

2. **Before Annas and Caiaphas: Peter's denials (18:12-27).** From the garden, Jesus is led to Annas, father-in-law of the high priest Caiaphas (whose unintended prophecy of Jesus' salvific death was noted in 11:50). Annas had an extraordinary career in the Jewish hierarchy. High priest himself from A.D. 7–14, he was succeeded in later years by five sons as well as by Caiaphas, a son-in-law. Not surprisingly, he remained a person of substantial power in Jerusalem, even though no longer high priest himself. In these verses the evangelist, as though utilizing a double stage, focuses the spotlight in turn on the Annas-Jesus discussion and then on the nearby encounters of Peter with his accusers.

Peter's first difficulty is at the very gate of the courtyard. Another disciple (the Beloved Disciple?) known to the high priest has used his influence to obtain entrance for Peter also. Peter is a mixture of courage—he is there following Jesus (v. 15)—and intense fear. At the challenge of a servant girl,

disciples, then about his teaching. ²⁰Jesus answered by saying:

"I have spoken publicly to any who would listen.
I always taught in a synagogue or in the temple area
where all the Jews come together.
There was nothing secret about anything I said.

²¹Why do you question me? Question those who heard me when I spoke. It should be obvious that they will know what I said." ²²At this reply, one of the guards who was standing nearby gave Jesus a sharp blow on the face. "Is that the way to answer the high priest?" he said. ²³Jesus replied, "If I said anything wrong produce the evidence, but if I spoke the truth why hit me?" ²⁴Annas next sent him, bound, to the high priest Caiaphas.

The Further Denials. ²⁵All through this, Simon Peter had been standing there warming himself. They said to him, "Are not you a disciple of his?" He denied it and said, "I am not!" ²⁶"But did I not see you with him in the garden?" insisted one of the high priest's slaves—as it happened, a relative of the man whose ear Peter had severed. ²⁷Peter denied it again. At that moment a cock began to crow.

The Trial before Pilate. ²⁸At daybreak they brought Jesus from Caiaphas to the

he capitulates. "Are you not one of this man's followers?" "Not I" (v. 17). The violence of Peter's sword has been transformed into the lying timidity of his tongue. Peter moves to the "charcoal fire" (v. 18). A chill has fallen on both body and spirit.

On the stage of a room apart (vv. 19-24), Peter's fear is being contrasted with Jesus' courage. Jesus' teaching has been out in the open, accessible "to any who would listen" ("to the world," in the Greek text). Why, then, is he questioned as though he were a conniving malefactor? A blow to the face is his answer. Annas, unable to gratify what seems to be cheap curiosity, sends Jesus, bound, to his son-in-law.

Meanwhile, back at the fire (vv. 25-27), Peter is slipping from bad to worse. Confronted by other bystanders and by a relative of the injured Malchus (v. 26), Peter, so courageous at the supper table (13:37), surrenders completely. "Are you not a disciple of his?" "I am not!" (v. 25). With the third denial, Peter strikes out—and a cock began to crow.

The details of Jesus' trials vary somewhat in the four Gospels. The arrest in a secluded place outside the city walls is a constant, but there is a variation regarding what happened after that. Where Mark 14:53-65 and Matt 26:57-68 speak of a formal night trial before the Sanhedrin, the religious governance in Jerusalem, Luke 22:54, 63-64 and John describe a less formal meeting that evening at the high priest's house, according to Luke, and with Annas, according to John. These discrepancies are the kind that would naturally arise as the accounts were passed along orally over the years. All four agree on some type of inquisition the following morning and on the definitive appearance before Pilate.

praetorium. They did not enter the praetorium themselves, for they had to avoid ritual impurity if they were to eat the Passover supper. [29]Pilate came out to them. "What accusation do you bring against this man?" he demanded. [30]"If he were not a criminal," they retorted, "we would certainly not have handed him over to you." [31]At this Pilate said, "Why do you not take him and pass judgment

3. Pilate: Condemnation (18:28-19:16). Pilate, as a historical character, is fairly well known. He ruled as Roman procurator of Judea, subordinate to the governor of Syria, for ten years (A.D. 26-36), during which time his chief duty was to administer finances and collect taxes for the imperial treasury. His treatment of the Jews was insensitive, frequently cruel. When his troops marched into Jerusalem with insignia bearing the image of Caesar, the Jews were incensed and persuaded him to have them removed only after a courageous and dangerous confrontation with the procurator in Caesarea, where his official residence was located. He also sequestered money from the temple funds with which he financed an aqueduct for Jerusalem. This caused another protest that terminated with violence as the protesting Jews were scattered by the clubs of Pilate's soldiers. His cruelty to the Samaritans resulted in their appeal to the Syrian governor, the legate Vitellus, who dismissed Pilate and sent him back to Rome to answer complaints before the emperor Tiberius. Tiberius, however, died before Pilate's arrival; and at that time Pilate disappears from history. The date of his death is unknown. (The early church historian Eusebius believed that he committed suicide.) A man of no great talent, he has entered history almost entirely because of his role in the death of Jesus.

Numerous commentators have noted that this trial before Pilate has been organized using the double-stage technique (*outside* with the crowd, *inside* with Jesus) and in the order of inverse parallelism (as was the case with the prologue). Schematically, we find the following seven scenes:

Outside	(a)	18:28-32:	Jewish authorities demand from Pilate the death of Jesus.
Inside	(b)	18:33-38a:	First dialogue between Pilate and Jesus.
Outside	(c)	18:38b-40:	Pilate wishes to release Jesus, since he finds him guilty of no crime.
Inside	(d)	19:1-3:	Flagellation and crowning with thorns: Jesus as king.
Outside	(c')	19:4-8:	Pilate finds Jesus guilty of no crime (twice).
Inside	(b')	19:9-11:	Second dialogue between Pilate and Jesus.
Outside	(a')	19:12-16:	Jewish authorities obtain from Pilate the sentence of death.

on him according to your law?" "We may not put anyone to death," the Jews answered. [32](This was to fulfill what Jesus had said indicating the sort of death he had to die.)

[33]Pilate went back into the praetorium and summoned Jesus. "Are you the King of the Jews?" he asked him. [34]Jesus answered, "Are you saying this on your own, or have others been telling you about me?" [35]"I am no Jew!" Pilate retorted. "It is your own people and the chief priests who have handed you over to me. What have you done?" [36]Jesus answered:

"My kingdom does not belong to this world.
If my kingdom were of this world, my subjects would be fighting
to save me from being handed over to the Jews.
As it is, my kingdom is not here."

[37]At this Pilate said to him, "So, then, you are a king?" Jesus replied:

"It is you who say I am a king.
The reason I was born,
the reason why I came into the world,
is to testify to the truth.

Clearly, and remarkably, (a), (b) and (c) are matched by (a'), (b') and (c'). Section (d) climactically stresses the kingship of Jesus. It is this ordering that we will follow as we study this section.

Outside (a) 18:28-32. John tells us nothing about Jesus' appearance before Caiaphas apart from the fact (18:24, 28). The praetorium (v. 28) was the official tribunal of the procurator while in Jerusalem. It is disputed as to whether it was located at the northwest corner of the temple area (the Antonia) or at Herod's palace on the western hill of the city. Mention of the avoidance of ritual impurity in order that they might eat the Passover supper (v. 28) informs us that John does *not* present the Last Supper as the paschal meal (13:1; 19:14, 31). The other three Gospels do. Commentators are far from agreeing upon any solution to this famous difficulty. The dialogue between Pilate and the authorities makes evident the intent of the latter to do away with Jesus, and it is Pilate who forces this admission (v. 31). The evangelist sees in this a fulfillment of the divine necessity that Jesus be lifted up (3:14; 8:28; 12:32-34) on the cross, a Roman punishment. What evidence we have lends credence to the statement in verse 31 that the Jerusalem Sanhedrin did not have authority to impose capital punishment, and especially while Pilate himself was in the city.

Inside (b) 18:33-38a. Pilate's question, "Are you the King of the Jews?" (v. 33), constitutes the first words of Pilate to Jesus also in Mark 15:2, Matt 27:11, and Luke 23:3. This supposes and constitutes strong proof that such an anti-Roman claim to kingship was the official accusation made against Jesus by the chief priests. Pilate's question was dangerous—an imprudent answer could bring condemnation as a revolutionary. Jesus' first response, consequently, is indirect, an appeal to Pilate's conscience (v. 34). But verses 36-37 are direct and to the point. Jesus is a king, but of a strikingly different

Anyone committed to the truth hears my voice." ³⁸"Truth!" said Pilate. "What does that mean?"

After this remark, Pilate went out again to the Jews and said to them: "Speaking for myself, I find no case against this man. ³⁹Recall your custom whereby I release someone to you at Passover time. Do you want me to release to you the king of the Jews?" ⁴⁰They shouted back, "We want Barabbas, not this one!" (Barabbas was an insurrectionist.)

19 ¹Pilate's next move was to take Jesus and have him scourged. ²The soldiers then wove a crown of thorns and fixed it on his head, throwing around his shoulders a cloak of royal purple. ³Repeatedly they came up to him and said, "All hail, king of the Jews!", slapping his face as they did so.

⁴Pilate went out a second time and said to the crowd: "Observe what I do. I am going to bring him out to you to make you realize that I find no case [against him]." ⁵When Jesus came out wearing the crown of thorns and the

type. His kingdom is not of this world (v. 36), not of earthly origin. In response to Pilate's following question, "So, then, you are a king?," Jesus answers that his whole mission is to witness to the truth. All who are committed to the truth hear his voice. The question up for judgment, insists Jesus, is whether or not one accepts him, truth incarnate (v. 37). Pilate stands in the shadow. He does not even understand the terms of the question (v. 38).

Outside (c) 18:38b-40. Out Pilate goes again, hoping this time that the choice of the crowd would free him from a decision he fears to make. Surely they will prefer to liberate Jesus rather than the criminal Barabbas (and, in so doing, liberate Pilate as well). But Pilate will not be let off the hook so lightly. "They shouted back, 'We want Barabbas'" (v. 40). Barabbas, says the Greek text, was a *lēistēs*, probably a political insurrectionist, although the term can also apply to an ordinary robber or bandit. The ball moves back into Pilate's court.

Inside (d) 19:1-3. John stresses here the elements of mockery that echo kingship—a kingship that Jesus truly possesses, but on a different level. Thus come the crown, the cloak of royal purple, the salutation as king. Ironically, notes John, he who was so thoroughly and diversely mocked as a king was truly king. It is this truth, stressed here in irony, that constitutes the theological and structural center of the trial before Pilate.

Outside (c') 19:4-8. This section parallels (c), Pilate's declaration of Jesus' innocence. In this instance Pilate states his opinion twice: "I find no case against him" (vv. 4, 6). Verse 6's "Take him and crucify him yourselves" is neither a condemnation nor a permission granted the accusers. A paraphrase might be: "Go ahead. Do it on your own and under your own responsibility, but don't expect me to be responsible for it." The answer to this reveals in all clarity the real reason for the antagonism of the local author-

purple cloak, Pilate said to them, "Look at the man!" ⁶As soon as the chief priests and the temple guards saw him they shouted, "Crucify him! Crucify him!" Pilate said, "Take him and crucify him yourselves; I find no case against him." ⁷"We have our law," the Jews responded, "and according to that law he must die because he made himself God's Son." ⁸When Pilate heard this kind of talk, he was more afraid than ever.

⁹Going back into the praetorium, he said to Jesus, "Where do you come from?" Jesus would not give him any answer. ¹⁰"Do you refuse to speak to me?" Pilate asked him. "Do you not know that I have the power to release you and the power to crucify you?" ¹¹Jesus answered:

"You would have no power over me whatever

unless it were given you from above.
That is why he who handed me over to you
is guilty of the greater sin."

¹²After this, Pilate was eager to release him, but the Jews shouted, "If you free this man you are no 'Friend of Caesar.' Anyone who makes himself a king becomes Caesar's rival." ¹³Pilate heard what they were saying, then brought Jesus outside and took a seat on a judge's bench at the place called the Stone Pavement—*Gabbatha* in Hebrew. ¹⁴(It was the Preparation Day for Passover, and the hour was about noon.) He said to the Jews, "Look at your king!" ¹⁵At this they shouted, "Away with him! Away with him! Crucify him!" "What!" Pilate exclaimed. "Shall I crucify your king?" The chief priests replied, "We have no

ities: ". . . according to that law he must die because he made himself *God's Son*" (v. 7). The Romans became involved because of a false accusation of kingship rivaling Caesar's; the Jewish accusation was that Jesus acted as the unique Son of God.

Inside (b') 19:9-11, the second dialogue. Pilate's reaction to this talk about Jesus' divine sonship is one of increasing fear and wonder. This is further increased, first by Jesus' silence (v. 9) and then by verse 11, the answer of a man confident of his own innocence and destiny.

Outside (a') 19:12-16. The condemnation is finally forced from Pilate by a return to the political accusation: "Anyone who makes himself a king becomes Caesar's rival" (v. 12). This accusation carries the day. The final scene shifts outside before the public, onto the stone pavement called Gabbatha. (An enormous pavement of huge worked stone lies evident today in the excavation of the Antonia at the corner of the old temple area.) The dialogue between Pilate and the crowd is kingly and ironic by Johannine intent. "Look at your king! . . . Shall I crucify your king?" (vv. 14-15). Back comes the dreadful confession of the chief priests: "We have no king but Caesar" (v. 15). This was blasphemy, for it was religious dogma that Yahweh and only Yahweh was king. John is telling us that those rejecting Jesus cannot have his Father as king. Pilate yields to political pressure and hands Jesus over. "It was the Preparation Day for the Passover, and the hour was about noon" (v. 14). As the Lamb of God (1:29, 36) is sentenced to

king but Caesar." ¹⁶In the end, Pilate handed Jesus over to be crucified.

Crucifixion and Death. Jesus was led away, and ¹⁷carrying the cross by himself, went out to what is called the Place of the Skull (in Hebrew, *Golgotha*). ¹⁸There they crucified him, and two others with him: one on either side, Jesus in the middle. ¹⁹Pilate had an inscription placed on the cross which read,

JESUS THE NAZOREAN
THE KING OF THE JEWS

²⁰This inscription, in Hebrew, Latin, and Greek, was read by many of the Jews, since the place where Jesus was crucified was near the city. ²¹The chief priests of the Jews tried to tell Pilate, "You should not have written, 'The King of the Jews.' Write instead, 'This man claimed to be King of the Jews.'" ²²Pilate answered, "What I have written, I have written."

²³After the soldiers had crucified Jesus they took his garments and divided them four ways, one for each soldier. There was also his tunic, but this tunic was woven in one piece from top to bottom and had no seam. ²⁴They said to each other, "We should not tear it. Let us throw dice to see who gets it." (The purpose of this was to have the Scripture fulfilled:

"They divided my garments among them;
for my clothing they cast lots.")

And this was what the soldiers did.

death, the Passover lambs are being readied for sacrifice. Mutually responsible for Jesus' death are Judas, a disciple; Pilate, a Roman; and the Jewish authorities of Jerusalem.

4. Crucifixion (19:16b-22). Jesus himself carries the cross (v. 17). John is not denying the assistance given by Simon of Cyrene—if, indeed, he knows of it—but is emphasizing the control of Jesus over his own life and death. He accepts his own death; he carries his own cross. He is crucified at the Place of the Skull (in Hebrew *Golgotha* and in Latin *Calvaria*, whence our "Calvary").

The inscription on the cross is mentioned, always with slight variations, by all four evangelists, but only John, who insists so much on Jesus' kingship, tells us of the three languages. Greek was the tongue of the Mediterranean world; Latin, that of the Roman empire. John is saying that Jesus' kingship is universal, proclaimed from the cross to the whole world. Pilate's stubborn insistence on leaving the inscription stand as written is his own bit of revenge against those who pressured him to condemn the innocent. Now let them squirm a little at a title that insults them.

5. Christ's clothing (19:23-24). This is the first of a series of incidents in which John sees the fulfillment of some Old Testament prophecy. The pitiful booty of Jesus' clothing is referred back to Ps 22:19, a psalm much used by the early church as a pre-shadowing of Jesus' passion. The reference to the seamless tunic *may* be a conscious parallel between Jesus and the high priest, whose robe was also seamless, but such a possibility is disputed by scholars. John speaks of Jesus, not as priest, but as king.

²⁵Near the cross of Jesus there stood his mother, his mother's sister, Mary the wife of Clopas, and Mary Magdalene. ²⁶Seeing his mother there with the disciple whom he loved, Jesus said to his mother, "Woman, there is your son." ²⁷In turn he said to the disciple, "There is your mother." From that hour onward, the disciple took her into his care.

²⁸After that, Jesus realizing that everything was now finished, said to fulfill the Scripture, "I am thirsty." ²⁹There was a

6. Jesus' mother and the Beloved Disciple (19:25-27). This scene, placed at the most important moment in the Gospel, must have more than simple filial significance, that is, the care of Jesus for his mother at the hour of his death. The only question is: What does this incident symbolize? Suggestions are numerous. Since this paragraph is set in the context of Jesus' delivering over his spirit (v. 30) and of the blood and water flowing from his pierced side (v. 34), I suggest that we find in these few verses John's symbolic picture of the birth of the Christian community. It is the hour of Jesus' glorification — his being lifted up — and as he dies, he hands over his Spirit. Beneath him stand a woman and a disciple, both unnamed as if to emphasize their symbolic character. The woman may well signify mother church, and the Beloved Disciple all disciples called to follow the loving obedience of their Lord. When to the mother-church woman and the Beloved Disciple figure are added the Spirit, which Jesus gives (v. 30) now that he has been glorified (7:39), and the blood and water, signs of the Eucharist and baptism, the Christian community stands revealed. This suggestion, though not certain, is not exaggerated, especially when working with an evangelist so theologically bi-leveled as John.

There may even be a subtle reference to the woman of Gen 3:15 and the enmity between her offspring and that of the Satan-serpent. John shows interest in the Book of Genesis. Starting his Gospel with the same initial phrase and a reference to creation, he presents a conflict between Satan and Jesus (12:31-33; 14:30), and speaks of Satan's offspring (Judas and the adversaries of 8:44). If the "woman" of 19:26 is, indeed, a reference to the woman of Gen 3:15, then John has reassembled all the elements of the Genesis story for a re-creation event: the serpent, the serpent's seed, the woman, the woman's seed and, perhaps, even the garden locale for "in the place where he had been crucified there was a garden" (19:41). Indeed, the crucifixion account not only ends in a garden (19:41) but also begins in one (18:1); and it is only John among the four evangelists who so locates it.

The Fourth Gospel may be presenting Mary beneath the cross in a double role:

a) *as feminine symbol of mother church*, caring for, and placed in the care of, Jesus' disciples, who become her children and, consequently, Jesus'

jar there, full of common wine. They stuck a sponge soaked in this wine on some hyssop and raised it to his lips. [30]When Jesus took the wine, he said, "Now it is finished." Then he bowed his head, and delivered over his spirit.

The Blood and Water. [31]Since it was the Preparation Day the Jews did not want to have the bodies left on the cross during the sabbath, for that sabbath was a solemn feast day. They asked Pilate that the legs be broken and the bodies be taken away. [32]Accordingly, the soldiers came and broke the legs of the men crucified with Jesus, first of the one, then of the other. [33]When they came to Jesus and saw that he was already dead, they did not break his legs. [34]One of the soldiers thrust a lance into his side, and immediately blood and water flowed out. [35](This testimony has been given by an eyewitness, and his testimony is true. He tells what he knows is true, so that you may believe.) [36]These events took place for the fulfillment of Scripture: "Break none of his bones."

brothers and sisters. Relation to Jesus is not merely individual; it includes a community, a family of brothers and sisters;

b) *as woman of the victory*, emphasizing the feminine contribution to salvation. The negative biblical portrait of Eva has been replaced by that of the life-giving Ave.

7. **Death (19:28-30).** For John, Jesus dies when he is ready to die, at the proper time, when Scripture has been fulfilled. The Scripture "I am thirsty" may refer to either Ps 69:21 or Ps 22:15. Both psalms are used often in the New Testament. The wine (v. 29) was the thin, bitter drink of the soldiers. The hyssop plant (v. 29) could hardly hold a sponge soaked with wine. It may enter here to recall to John's Jewish readers the plant that sprinkled Israelite doors with the saving blood of the Passover lamb in Exod 12:22. If so, it is intimately connected with what follows. "Now it is finished" (v. 30) — accomplished is the work Jesus had to do, the will of his Father, the Scriptures, the salvation of humankind. "Then he bowed his head, and *delivered over* the spirit" (v. 30). This wording is unique, proper to the Fourth Gospel. Jesus' death-glorification has released the Spirit into the world (7:39; 19:34; 20:22).

8. **The lance (19:31-37).** The urgency apparent in verse 31 arises from the fact that it is Friday afternoon, with the Sabbath (also Passover for John) beginning at sundown. There were but a few hours left for what would necessarily be done to the bodies. The legs of the other two, consequently, were broken to hasten their death, but this was useless for Jesus, already dead. Instead, his side was pierced, releasing a mixture of blood and water, to which the evangelist, or his source of information, bears testimony as an eyewitness. Verse 35 emphasizes this fact. Many of the church fathers have seen in the blood and water signs of the Eucharist and baptism, the life sources of the church, the new Eve, coming forth from the side of the new

[37]There is still another Scripture passage which says:

"They shall look on him whom they have pierced."

Burial. [38]Afterward, Joseph of Arimathea, a disciple of Jesus (although a secret one for fear of the Jews), asked Pilate's permission to remove Jesus' body. Pilate granted it, so they came and took the body away. [39]Nicodemus (the man who had first come to Jesus at night) likewise came, bringing a mixture of myrrh and aloes which weighed about a hundred pounds. [40]They took Jesus' body, and in accordance with Jewish burial custom bound it up in wrappings of cloth with perfumed oils. [41]In the place where he had been crucified there was a garden, and in the garden a new tomb in which no one had ever been buried. [42]Because of the Jewish Preparation Day they buried Jesus there, for the tomb was close at hand.

Adam. John refers again to fulfillment of Old Testament passages. "Break none of his bones" is a fusion of Exod 12:46, which concerns the paschal lamb, and Ps 34:20, which describes God's protection of the just man. "They shall look on him whom they have pierced" refers to Zech 12:10, where the piercing is joined to God's pouring out on the inhabitants of Jerusalem a spirit of grace and petition. The piercing of Jesus does even more.

9. The burial (19:38-42). All four evangelists mention the participation of Joseph of Arimathea in Jesus' burial (Matt 27:57-60; Mark 16:43-46; Luke 23:50-53). Only Matt 27:60, however, explains how it was that the new tomb was available for use—it belonged to Joseph. And only John introduces Nicodemus. For John, both men were crypto-Christians breaking free from the darkness of their fear. Their courageous act is a verification of John 12:32: ". . . and I—once I am lifted up from the earth—will draw all men to myself."

The huge amount of myrrh and aloes (v. 39) used for the burial may be one final Johannine reference to Jesus' kingship. He receives a regal burial.

20:1-31 The Resurrection

Here, as in chapter 9, the text is arranged in dramatic form (next page), as it might be if performed by actors and actresses. The number of participants could be reduced by having only one angel (A) and one disciple (D). The surprising and challenging fact is that John's text lends itself so naturally to such dramatic arrangement.

[ACT I: The Tomb

Scene 1: *Sunday morning.* Mary Magdalene (*MM*), Peter (*P*), Beloved Disciple (*BD*), Narrator (*N*)]

> *N:* ¹Early in the morning on the first day of the week, while it was still dark,
>
> *MM:* Mary Magdalene came to the tomb. She saw that the stone had been moved away, ²so she ran off to Simon Peter and the other disciple
>
> *N:* (the one Jesus loved)
>
> *MM:* and told them, "The Lord has been taken from the tomb! We don't know where they have put him!"
>
> *P:* ³At that, Peter
>
> *N:* and the other disciple
>
> *P and BD:* started out on their way toward the tomb.
>
> *N:* ⁴They were running side by side,
>
> *BD:* but then the other disciple outran Peter and reached the tomb first. ⁵He did not enter but bent down to peer in, and saw the wrappings lying on the ground.
>
> *P:* ⁶Presently, Simon Peter came along behind him and entered the tomb. He observed the wrappings on the ground ⁷and saw the piece of cloth which had covered the head not lying with the wrappings, but rolled up in a place by itself.
>
> *BD:* ⁸Then the disciple who had arrived first at the tomb went in. He saw and believed.
>
> *N:* ⁹Remember, as yet they did not understand the Scripture that Jesus had to rise from the dead.
>
> *P and BD:* ¹⁰With this, the disciples went back home.

[**Scene 2:** *The same Sunday morning.* Mary Magdalene (*MM*), Angels (*AA*), Jesus (*J*), Disciples, Narrator (*N*)]

> *N:* ¹¹Meanwhile, Mary stood weeping
>
> *MM:* beside the tomb. Even as she wept, she stooped to peer inside, ¹²and there she saw two angels in dazzling robes.
>
> *A-1:* One was seated at the head
>
> *A-2:* and the other at the foot of the place where Jesus' body had lain.
>
> *AA:* ¹³"Women," they asked her, "why are you weeping?"
>
> *MM:* She answered them, "Because the Lord has been taken away, and I do not know where they have put him."
>
> *N:* ¹⁴She had no sooner said this
>
> *MM:* than she turned around and caught sight of Jesus standing there.
>
> *N:* But she did not know him.
>
> *J:* ¹⁵"Woman," he asked her, "why are you weeping? Who is it you are looking for?"
>
> *MM:* She supposed he was the gardener, so she said, "Sir, if you are the one who carried him off, tell me where you have laid him and I will take him away."
>
> *J:* ¹⁶Jesus said to her, "Mary!"
>
> *MM:* She turned to him and said (in Hebrew), "Rabbouni!"
>
> *N:* (meaning "Teacher").

J: ¹⁷Jesus then said: "Do not cling to me, for I have not yet ascended to the Father. Rather, go to my brothers and tell them, 'I am ascending to my Father and your Father, to my God and your God!'"

MM: ¹⁸Mary Magdalene went to the disciples. "I have seen the Lord!" she announced. Then she reported what he said to her.

[ACT II: The Upper Room

Scene 1: *That Sunday evening.* Disciples (*DD*), Jesus (*J*), Thomas (*Th*), Narrator (*N*)]

N: ¹⁹On the evening of that first day of the week,
D-1: even though the disciples had locked the doors of the place
D-2: where they were for fear of the Jews,
J: Jesus came and stood before them. "Peace be with you," he said. ²⁰When he had said this, he showed them his hands and his side.
DD: At the sight of the Lord the disciples rejoiced.
J: ²¹"Peace be with you," he said again. "As the Father has sent me, so I send you."
N: ²²Then he breathed on them and said:
J: "Receive the Holy Spirit. ²³If you forgive men's sins, they are forgiven them; if you hold them bound, they are held bound."
Th: ²⁴It happened that one of the Twelve, Thomas
N: (the name means "Twin"),
Th: was absent when Jesus came.
DD: ²⁵The other disciples kept telling him: "We have seen the Lord!"
Th: His answer was, "I will never believe it without probing the nail-prints in his hands, without putting my finger in the nail-marks and my hand into his side."

[Scene 2: *One week later.* Disciples (*DD*), Jesus (*J*), Thomas (*Th*), Narrator (*N*)]

N: ²⁶A week later,
DD: the disciples were once more in the room,
Th: and this time Thomas was with them.
N: Despite the locked doors,
J: Jesus came and stood before them. "Peace be with you," he said; ²⁷then, to Thomas: "Take your finger and examine my hands. Put your hand into my side. Do not persist in your unbelief, but believe!"
Th: ²⁸Thomas said in response, "My Lord and my God!"
J: ²⁹Jesus then said to him: "You became a believer because you saw me. Blest are they who have not seen and have believed."
N: ³⁰Jesus performed many other signs as well—signs not recorded here—in the presence of his disciples. ³¹But these have been recorded to help you believe that
All: JESUS IS THE MESSIAH, THE SON OF GOD,
N: so that through this faith you may have life in his name.

1. Literary arrangement. John has composed this chapter with artistic care. Act I is located at the tomb, where the two different incidents (scenes) occur. Act II takes place in the room, the two scenes occurring one week apart. Each scene has two main characters: Peter and the Beloved Disciple;

Mary Magdalene and Jesus; Jesus and the disciples; Jesus and Thomas. As we advance through the four scenes, a minor character in one (Mary, then the disciples, finally Thomas) becomes a major one in the following. All is tightly coordinated, neatly orchestrated. In schematic form, with the italicized names being the main characters in the scene, we find:

ACT I **Tomb**	**Scene 1** (Sun. a.m.)	Mary M., *Peter, Beloved Disciple*
	Scene 2 (Same Sun. a.m.)	*Mary M.*, 2 angels, *Jesus*, disciples
ACT II **Tomb**	**Scene 1** (Same Sun. p.m.)	*Jesus, disciples*, Thomas
	Scene 2 (Sun. 1 week later)	*Jesus, Thomas*, disciples

2. Theological intent. John's theology becomes evident through observing the reactions of the participants. How do they arrive at belief in the risen Lord? In the opening scene, Mary, a minor character, sees the stone moved from the tomb. Her reaction is the natural one: "The Lord has been taken from the tomb" (v. 2). She does not yet believe.

Peter and the Beloved Disciple, the central actors, proceed to the tomb with haste (and hope). They see the burial clothes and head wrapping. Peter remains perplexed, but the response of the Beloved Disciple is one of faith. "He saw and believed" (v. 8). This loved and loving disciple saw only the minimum yet believed.

In the following scene (vv. 11-18), Mary now becomes a major character. She still holds the natural explanation (vv. 13, 15 repeat the substance of v. 2). She comes to faith only when she has heard (v. 16) and seen the Lord (v. 18). Jesus' sheep recognize his voice (10:4).

The disciples, introduced in Scene 2, become central in the scene that follows (vv. 19-25). Beginning in a state of fear, they pass from fear to joy "at the sight of the Lord" (v. 20). For them, too, faith comes through seeing.

Thomas, a minor character in verses 19-25, becomes central in the final scene. His stance is one of extreme incredulity. He will not believe unless he sees and touches (v. 25). And so Jesus invites him to faith through sight and touch (v. 27).

The evangelist is reviewing all these varying reactions and possibilities *for people of his own time.* What will be their reaction, continued reaction, to the resurrection? Will it be the perplexity of Peter? Will it be that of the Beloved Disciple, who, united so intimately with his Lord in love, believed immediately with minimum evidence? Will it be that of Mary Magdalene and the other disciples, who believed only when they saw and heard? Will they be like Thomas, who refused to believe unless he saw and touched, unless placed in a position in which unbelief became impossible? The evangelist is saying to his own fellow Christians: "Those first disciples were by no means exemplary, nor was their situation so fortunate. Faith was almost forced upon them. That is not something to be envied. Our own situation can be more positive, more profitable, more Christian. Let us follow the example of the Beloved Disciple, who believed with such little evidence. We can be gifted with the ninth beatitude: 'Blest are they who have not seen and have believed' (v. 29). And indeed, blest are we who, without seeing, *believe in the risen Jesus, our Lord and our God.*"

3. Specific verses. *Verse 2:* "The Lord has been taken from the tomb!" John knows this natural explanation, probably from controversies with non-Christians (Matt 28:13-15). He also denies it. The burial clothes were found, and in order (vv. 6-7), which would hardly be the case if someone had taken the body. These clothes are intentionally similar to those of Lazarus (ch. 11), who, however, came forth still wrapped in his. Resurrection is different.

Verse 8: "He saw and believed." The singular "He" limits this to the Beloved Disciple. Intensity of love leads to instant belief. It is this same love that will enable him to recognize the Lord in 21:4, 7 when the others do not.

Verse 9: This verse alludes again to the process by which the post-resurrection disciples interpreted Jesus' life by means of the Old Testament Scripture (John 2:17, 22; 12:16).

Verse 14: "But she did not know him." The various resurrection accounts accent this phenomenon, that the risen Lord was truly Jesus of Nazareth, *the same but different.* He passes through locked doors (20:19, 26) and is unrecognized by personal friends (by Mary here, by the disciples in 21:4, by the Emmaus pair in Luke 24:16). The Lord *is* recognized, however, by the sound of his voice (Mary in v. 16); by love (the Beloved Disciple in 20:8 and 21:7); in the breaking of bread (Luke 24:30-31); and in the power of God's written word (Luke 24:32). All these elements are integral to community liturgy.

Verse 16: "Jesus said to her, 'Mary!'" This should remind us of 10:4. Jesus' sheep recognize his voice.

Verse 17: "Do not cling to me, for I have not yet ascended to the Father." The meaning is difficult to ascertain. Is it that Jesus is at that moment enroute to the Father and Mary is seen to delay the passage? Or that she clings to his feet *in worship* (as in Matt 28:9), whereas Jesus' humanity will become the glorified center of worship (the new temple) only after his ascension, with its fulfillment of his glorification?

". . . to my Father and your Father, to my God and your God" could stress the difference between Jesus' relationship to the Father and ours. But it can also do just the opposite, indicating that Jesus' Father is truly ours, that his God is our God also.

Verse 20: "At the sight of the Lord the disciples rejoiced." In the context of the "little while—short time" passage of 16:22, the disciples were told: ". . . you are sad for a time, but I shall see you again; then your hearts *will rejoice* . . . ." Our present verse, 20:20, is the fulfillment. Jesus has returned, already returned, through his resurrection and through his gift of the Spirit in verse 22.

Verses 21-22 are a key passage in Johannine theology. The disciples receive the Holy Spirit at this second coming of Jesus: the *eschaton*, the final era, is now; future is present. In 7:39, the Spirit had not yet been given, since Jesus was not yet glorified. On the cross, Jesus, manifesting the nature of God, which is love, delivers over the Spirit (19:30), symbolized immediately afterward by the flow of the sacramental symbols of blood and water. And now, at his first encounter with the believing community, he breathes the Spirit again as he celebrates the re-creation of God's people. Simultaneously, he sends out these disciples just as the Father had sent him (v. 21). His mission becomes theirs; his work is placed in their hands. And that mission, that work, is to manifest God who is love in their words and deeds. Through them now, enlivened by the Spirit, will the presence of God become known and seen and felt in the world. If in truth Jesus is God's sacrament, God's exegete, we in turn through the Spirit become Jesus' sacraments, his living exegetes.

Verses 22-23, which speak clearly of the community's share in Jesus' power to forgive sins, can be simply a reference to baptism, the traditional sacrament of forgiveness, or to the church's continuous preaching of forgiveness of sins in Jesus. But this reference to sharing in Jesus' power probably intends more than that. Through the ever-present Spirit, the Christian community can offer a restored union with Father and Son, a divine indwelling that creates peace (v. 21) with God and neighbor. Over the centuries, Christian communities have developed different means by which this unifying power is put into effect.

Verse 24: Only in the Fourth Gospel does Thomas receive any emphasis (11:16; 14:5; 20:24-28; 21:2). A historical character, he also functions in this Gospel as a character-type. He is a combination of seeming courage (11:16) and ignorance (14:5), but especially is he a stubborn seeker of manifest resurrection credentials. Surely he calls to mind and reflects, for the evangelist, fellow Christians in the community who, beneath a courageous exterior, manifest both ignorance and lack of deep faith. To all such, Jesus and John say: "Do not persist in your unbelief, but believe" (v. 27).

Verse 28: "My Lord and my God!" There is no doubt that John intends this powerful phrasing (Ps 35:23-24) as a, or better *the*, Christian profession of faith. For the Johannine disciple, Jesus is both Lord and God. With this profession, John creates his own inclusion to the Gospel, the corresponding covers to his book of good news; for "My Lord and my God" at the conclusion corresponds to the opening ". . . and the Word was God" (1:1). The two statements are intentionally parallel.

Verses 30-31 are quite clearly a conclusion, the ending to the original edition of the Gospel. What the evangelist has written — which is not all that he could have written — is meant to urge and strengthen belief in Jesus as the Christ — and as the Son of God. John has already given us this profession in 11:27 on the lips of Martha in the context of another raising from the dead. To live, to really live, is to believe this: that Jesus of Nazareth is indeed the Messiah. And more, he is truly God's Son, dependent on the Father and obedient to him, yet himself divine. He is the Christian's Lord; he is the Christian's God.

D. EPILOGUE: APPEARANCE IN GALILEE

John 21:1-25

This final chapter is an addition to an original Gospel version that concluded with the magnificent statement of 20:31. It is found, however, in every ancient manuscript of the Gospel that we possess and must have been appended almost with the original publication of the work. Added by an expert in John's thought — surely by one of his disciples — and by one thoroughly conversant with the Gospel material, it is a genuine part of the canonical Gospel.

Chapter 21 has been tied to the previous chapters by a host of literary and theological links. Johannine characteristics found in this chapter are the Sea of Tiberias in verse 1; the names of Simon Peter, Thomas the Twin, Nathanael from Cana in verse 2; the night-day contrast of verses 3-4; the lack of recognition in verse 4; the Beloved Disciple of verse 7, who relates to Peter and who first recognizes the Lord; the charcoal fire of verse 9, together with the image of Jesus as servant and giver of bread to the disciples; the reference in verse 14 to two previous appearances (in ch. 20); Peter's triple profession (vv. 15-17) to counterbalance the triple denial and to reintroduce the shepherd theme (ch. 10); the glorifying aspect of Peter's death in verse 19; the reference to the Beloved Disciple's position next to Jesus at the Last Supper in verse 20. If this chapter is an addition — and it is — it is nonetheless a beautiful addition, and the Christian community would be considerably poorer without it.

IV. APPENDIX:
THE RESURRECTION APPEARANCE
IN GALILEE

21 **The Fishermen.** ¹Later, at the Sea of Tiberias, Jesus showed himself to the disciples [once again]. This is how the appearance took place. ²Assembled were Simon Peter, Thomas ("the Twin"), Nathanael (from Cana in Galilee), Zebedee's sons, and two other disciples. ³Simon Peter said to them, "I am going out to fish." "We will join you," they replied, and went off to get into their boat. All through the night they caught nothing. ⁴Just after daybreak Jesus was standing on the shore, though none of the disciples knew it was Jesus. ⁵He said to them, "Children, have you caught anything to eat?" "Not a thing," they answered. ⁶"Cast your net off to the starboard side," he suggested, "and you will find something." So they made a cast, and took so many fish they could not haul the net in. ⁷Then the disciple Jesus loved cried out to Peter, "It is the Lord!" On hearing it was the Lord, Simon Peter threw on some clothes—he was stripped—and jumped into the water.

⁸Meanwhile the other disciples came in the boat, towing the net full of fish. Actually they were not far from land—no more than a hundred yards. ⁹When they landed, they saw a charcoal fire there with a fish laid on it and some bread. ¹⁰"Bring some of the fish

1. The catch of fish (21:1-14). This story may well be the same as that recounted in Luke 5:4-10. Luke purposely limits Christ's resurrection activities to the area of Jerusalem, so he placed this Galilee story in chapter 5 of his Gospel for its rich homiletic advantage. Called to be fishers of men and women, the disciples can catch nothing without the assistance of the Lord. And indeed, Peter's confession in Luke 5:8, "Leave me, Lord. I am a sinful man," makes more sense if this was originally a post-resurrection story following Peter's denials.

The Sea of Tiberias (v. 1) is a Johannine locale (6:22-23), and the fishing companions are, in general, already known to us, with the exception of "Zebedee's sons," who here make their only appearance in the Fourth Gospel. Among the "two other disciples," seemingly, is the Beloved Disciple, who appears unexpectedly in verse 7. The lack of success during the night, followed by enormous success with the daylight presence of Jesus (vv. 3-6), is a practical application of John's frequent comments about night and day, light and darkness. The disciples' failure to recognize Jesus reminds us of a similar failure on the part of Mary (20:14), and we are hardly surprised when the Beloved Disciple is the first to recognize the Lord (v. 7).

The charcoal fire (v. 9) serves a double purpose. It sets the scene for Jesus' servant role as he becomes giver of bread (and fish) to the disciples and also serves as a stage prop for Peter's profession of love, recalling the previous charcoal fire (18:18), next to which Peter had denied the Lord.

The mention of precisely 153 fish (v. 11) has led to symbolic interpretations of all kinds. And indeed, there must be symbolism involved. John hardly means that the disciples took time out to make a count that then

you just caught," Jesus told them. ¹¹Simon Peter went aboard and hauled ashore the net loaded with sizable fish — one hundred fifty-three of them! In spite of the great number, the net was not torn. ¹²"Come and eat your meal," Jesus told them. Not one of the disciples presumed to inquire, "Who are you?" for they knew it was the Lord. ¹³Jesus came over, took the bread and gave it to them, and did the same with the fish. ¹⁴This marked the third time that Jesus appeared to the disciples after being raised from the dead.

Peter the Shepherd. ¹⁵When they had eaten their meal, Jesus said to Simon Peter, "Simon, son of John, do you love me more than these?" "Yes, Lord," he said, "you know that I love you." At which Jesus said, "Feed my lambs."
¹⁶A second time he put his question, "Simon, son of John, do you love me?" "Yes, Lord," Peter said, "you know that I love you." Jesus replied, "Tend my sheep."
¹⁷A third time Jesus asked him, "Simon, son of John, do you love me?" Peter was hurt because he had asked a third time, "Do you love me?" So he said

became part of Christian tradition. Saint Jerome believed that the zoology of his time taught that there were 153 different kinds of fish; and the number, as a result, reflected universality. Jerome was probably incorrect about the zoologists of his own day, but his suspicion of some universal symbolism was probably correct. Others have arrived at the same kind of symbolism by pointing out, for what it is worth, that 153 is a "universal" number, the sum of a triangle of increasing lines of dots whose tip is one and whose base is seventeen.

Another symbolic possibility at this point is drawn from the fact that the disciples bring the catch (humankind) to the meal (Eucharist) prepared by the risen Lord.

This appearance is Jesus' third (v. 14), when added to the two "room" appearances of chapter 20.

2. Peter (21:15-19). This encounter of Peter with his risen Lord is filled with beautiful material. Jesus offers Peter a public opportunity to profess repentance through love, surely a striking example of what it is that reestablishes our relationship with the Lord after sin. Peter's threefold denial is balanced by this threefold profession of love (the charcoal fire is the visible stage link). With this, he and his Lord are "at-oned."

This incident is also a continuation of the shepherd theme of chapter 10. There seems to be no real difference between Jesus' three commands:

"*Feed* my lambs";

"Tend my *sheep*," to which is added the composite

"*Feed* my *sheep*."

The function of Yahweh-shepherd in Ezek 34 passes to Jesus-shepherd in John 10 to Peter-shepherd in John 21. It is important to note how Peter's shepherd role is tied to love (vv. 15-17) and to a willingness (like the good

to him: "Lord, you know everything. You know well that I love you." Jesus said to him, "Feed my sheep.

¹⁸ "I tell you solemnly:
as a young man
you fastened your belt
and went about as you pleased;
but when you are older
you will stretch out your hands,
and another will tie you fast
and carry you off against your will."

¹⁹(What he said indicated the sort of death by which Peter was to glorify God.) When Jesus had finished speaking he said to him, "Follow me."

The Beloved Disciple. ²⁰Peter turned around at that, and noticed that the disciple whom Jesus loved was following (the one who had leaned against Jesus' chest during the supper and said, "Lord, which one will hand you over?"). ²¹Seeing him, Peter was prompted to ask Jesus, "But Lord, what about him?" ²²"Suppose I want him to stay until I come," Jesus replied, "how does that concern you? Your business is to follow me." ²³This is how the report spread among the brothers that this disciple was not going to die. Jesus never told him, as a matter of fact, that the disciple was not going to die; all he said was, "Suppose I

shepherd of 10:11-18) to lay down his life (vv. 18-19). Note, too, how Peter's laying down his life glorified God, as did that of Jesus. Love, love to the limit, selfless, life-giving love manifests (glorifies) God because that is God's nature. An act of selfless, life-giving love is God's name published before the world.

When this chapter was written, Peter's death was already an accomplished fact. Like his Lord (note the "Follow me" of v. 22), he had already stretched out his hands (v. 18) to die on Vatican hill. The tying fast (v. 18) would be the fastening to the cross, always accomplished in part by ropes.

3. The Beloved Disciple (20:20-23). This final incident centers, fittingly, on the Beloved Disciple. The question is: What about him? (v. 21). Verse 23 makes sense only if a belief that the Beloved Disciple would live to see Jesus' final coming had been shattered by his unexpected death. As his followers— among whom was the author of this chapter—looked back to recall the source of their misguided belief, they could discover only an ambiguous statement of Jesus upon which this erroneous concept had been based: "Suppose I want him to stay until I come, how does that concern you?" (v. 22). The mystery of the Beloved Disciple's life and death was not theirs to comprehend. His hour, like the Lord's, had come, leaving them behind. The important thing for the moment, says verse 24, is that this disciple remains on as the eyewitness testimony on which the written Gospel is based. It was he who wrote—or caused to write, like Pilate in 19:22—this version of the good news. The "we know" indicates that this chapter itself has been written by others, that it is a God-sent addition.

Verse 25 concludes the chapter with a brief statement that cannot match in content the magnificent original conclusion of 20:30-31. The reader

want him to stay until I come [how does that concern you]?"
Conclusion. 24It is this same disciple who is the witness to these things; it is he who wrote them down and his testimony, we know, is true. 25There are still many other things that Jesus did, yet if they were written about in detail, I doubt there would be room enough in the entire world to hold the books to record them.

should be encouraged to re-read that beautiful finale as one finishes the reading and studying and praying of this impressive presentation of the Good News that is Jesus, God's revelation, God's love manifested in self-sacrifice, and for us the sole way and truth and life.

Having studied chapter 21, we can now hazard a guess as to why it was added to the original Gospel. There are two centers of attention in the chapter. The first is Peter, who is successively reconciled through his profession of love, then constituted the shepherd, and finally described as a martyr whose death glorified God. The second is the Beloved Disciple, whose death has deeply disturbed the community, but whose eyewitness testimony remains the secure foundation of its faith. This chapter has taken origin from these two concerns: to paint a portrait of Peter as the reconciled, loving, and martyred community shepherd, and to base the faith of the community in the Beloved Disciple on firmer footing. All-important for the Christians is not the Beloved Disciple's visible presence but his life-giving word. And this is enclosed forever in this Gospel.

CONCLUSIONS TO OUR STUDY OF JOHN'S GOSPEL

Now that we have finished our study of John's Gospel, it might be of help to attempt a brief résumé of some of the more important issues regarding the theology, literary origin, and community background of the Gospel.

1. Revelation. John's central theological teaching concerns revelation: God's revelation of himself in his completely unique Son, Jesus of Nazareth, one with the Father, the living and incarnate Word, who in himself bespeaks, proclaims, identifies, immediates the Father. To know Jesus is to know God. And so, too, John gives us the Book of Glory, which climaxes in the ultimate revelation of the Son as self-sacrificing love. It is on the cross that Jesus glorifies/manifests the Father. God the Father, therefore, is love. This will be the final, simple, concise definition of 1 John 4:16, "God is love, and he who abides in love abides in God, and God in him."

2. Mission. To reveal the Father is Jesus' mission; it is for this that he has been sent. This mission is, in turn, passed to us who believe in him. Our Christian mission is to reveal both the Father and the Son within us. God who is love, the Son who lays down his life, will be known only through us, through our lives of self-sacrificing love. The baton of the Word-made-flesh has been passed to us, who are now called to reveal the Word through our flesh. Only in this way will the world come to know and to believe. Since all Christians are called equally to share in this mission, John ceaselessly speaks of "disciples — *mathētai*." John's Christianity is very egalitarian: his challenge is a question to us all. Do we, or do we not, reveal the God who is love?

3. Paraclete. In this mission we are not alone. To us has been given the Paraclete, both to enliven and to enlighten us. As Jesus is God-with-us (Matthew's Emmanuel), so the Spirit is Christ-with-us. He appears as Jesus leaves. He is delivered over as Jesus dies on the cross, breathed upon the disciples at Jesus' first resurrection appearance to them, sent from above as Jesus returns to his Father's side. Every step in Jesus' exaltation is accompanied by a gift to us of his Spirit.

4. The Beloved Disciple. If it is the Paraclete's function to enlighten and enliven the disciples, the community of the Fourth Gospel has experienced this in a particular way through the effect of the Spirit on the Beloved Disciple. It is he who, as eyewitness, provides the firm basis for the belief of the community. As the Word can reveal the Father, since he is at the Father's bosom (1:18), so the Beloved Disciple can reveal the Son, since he rested at the Son's bosom (13:25).

Appearing possibly in 1:35-40 as the anonymous of the two disciples, the Beloved Disciple makes frequent appearances starting with the passion material: at the Last Supper in 13:23-25; very probably in the high priest's courtyard as the other disciple of 18:15-16; at the foot of the cross as Jesus is glorified and the Christian community comes into being (19:25-27); at the tomb (20:1-10); and, finally, during the fishing trip of 21:7, 20-24.

The Beloved Disciple seems to be a Jerusalem disciple with connections to the high priest. His presentation of Jesus — on the solid presumption that he either authored the Fourth Gospel or was extremely instrumental in shaping its literary form (19:35; 21:24) — is so different from that of the other three Gospels that he was hardly one of the Twelve, a title he rarely uses (only in 6:67-71 and 20:24). He is coupled with Peter, over whom he has a certain kind of spiritual precedence. Peter asks Jesus through him (13:24); Peter knows Jesus through him (21:7); Peter believes after him (20:8).

At this present moment of scholarship, it seems best to accept the Beloved Disciple as anonymous, yet as a true disciple and eyewitness of the Lord, connected with Jerusalem, not one of the Twelve, whose different background and different Christian experience led him to produce, directly or indirectly, a version of the Good News strikingly different from that of Mark, Matthew, and Luke.

Historical as he is, the Beloved Disciple is also presented to us as an ideal, a model of what we should be as disciples ourselves—loved and loving.

5. John's community. One very striking facet of the Fourth Gospel is the manner in which the life of John's own community interpenetrates that of Jesus. Since Jesus lives on through and in his Spirit, the Paraclete, the life and history of John's community continue to be the life and history of the risen Lord. What happens to the community happens to Jesus. What is spoken by the Paraclete-enlivened disciples is spoken by Jesus, for the Paraclete transmits what he hears Jesus saying (16:13). Jewish controversies with John's group become controversies with Jesus, and what Jesus says is the community's response. This is Gospel writing and, clearly, not modern history. Let us note three of the most obvious instances. At the end of chapter 6, the sharp discussion regarding the consumption of Jesus' flesh and blood is a later Johannine controversy. In chapter 8, the controversy between Jesus and the Pharisees concerning his unique Sonship and identification as the I AM is, historically speaking, a controversy between the later Pharisees and John's community. A third is apparent in chapter 9, where the blind man excommunicated from the synagogue represents Johannine Jewish Christians of the eighties–nineties, for whom profession of faith in Jesus means radical excommunication from religion, family, and friends. The Jesus of the Fourth Gospel speaks differently from the Jesus of the first three Gospels because his voice is so frequently transmitted through the lips of the Paraclete-inspired community.

If it is true that the Gospel reflects John's own community, we can identify this community as a group that includes (1) true Israelites, such as Nathanael (1:47) and previous followers of the Baptist (1:35) and the man born blind (ch. 9), all of whom have become disciples out of Judaism; (2) Greeks, such as those of 12:20-22; (3) Samaritans who, white for the harvest, have recognized Jesus as Savior (4:42).

This community is in uneasy relationship with the unbelieving world; with the Pharisees, who reject Jesus' claims (chs. 7-8); even with other Christians who are deficient in their Eucharistic belief (6:66) or who remain crypto-Christians out of fear of expulsion from the synagogue and Judaism (12:42-43).

It is also a community that, while recognizing the importance of the Twelve in general (6:67-70) and of Peter in particular (1:42; 6:68-69; 21:15-19), places its main emphasis on discipleship and the presence of the Paraclete.

6. Dramatic elements. This combination of Beloved Disciple, community, and Paraclete has, for some as yet unexplained reasons, given us a Gospel that is amazingly rich in dramatic techniques. Chapters such as 4, 9, 11, and 20 can be given instant staging. Peter, Thomas, Philip, and Judas (chs. 13–14) are present simply to ask leading questions that help to carry the discussion forward. Other characters, historical as they are, model roles. Nathanael (1:47) is what all true Israelites should be. Andrew and Philip (1:41, 45; 6:5-9; 12:20-22) perform like real missionaries. Nicodemus portrays a person who passes gradually, though with fear, from darkness into light (3:1-10; 7:50-52; 19:39). The Samaritan woman (ch. 4) clarifies the possibility, for a woman as for a man, to move from sin and ignorance into faith and mission. Jesus' mother models Mother Church. The Beloved Disciple portrays what all disciples should be.

The Gospel is filled with other dramatic elements, too: with frequent irony as the obviously untrue turns out to be eminently true – Jesus *will* die for the whole world (11:52) and he really is king (19:19-22); with the use of ambiguity, misunderstanding, clarification to captivate the interest of the hearers; with an almost pre-play program description of Jesus in chapter 1; with the stage props of the bucket of the Samaritan woman (4:28) and Peter's charcoal fire (18:18; 21:9).

All of this helps to make this Gospel so rich that a lifetime of study cannot plumb its depths. As Christians of the past twenty centuries have written about the Fourth Gospel without coming close to exhausting its riches, so, it seems certain, will Christians of the next twenty as well.

The First Epistle of John

Text and Commentary

Tucked far away from the Fourth Gospel in our Bible lie the three writings called the Epistles of John. It is to these that our attention must now turn. As was done with the Gospel, we shall postpone a consideration of what are usually treated as introductory questions (author, occasion, date, community, theological content, interrelationship of the three epistles) until we have actually encountered the material that provides what answers there are to such problems. The only introductory issue we want to face here is that of the possible division of the First Epistle of John. This is a difficult and confusing question, since the epistle is repetitious and circular — like a spiral, suggest some authors, which goes round and round but with a definite, even if not too distinguishable, progression. Though commentators differ in their breakdown of the material, there is sufficient consensus to propose the following division as workable. Though admittedly very general, it will help the reader both to distinguish diverse elements and to synthesize them into an overall unity.

PROLOGUE:	1:1-4	The historical reality of the Christian message
	1:5–2:2	Walking in the light: the question of sin
	2:3-17	Keeping the commandments (accent on love)
	2:18-27	Warning against false teachers, the antichrists (accent on faith)
	2:28–3:24	Children of God, children of the devil, love versus hatred
	4:1-6	The two spirits
	4:7-21	God's love inspires ours
	5:1-13	Faith: conclusion
EPILOGUE:	5:14-21	Prayer for sinners, summary

PROLOGUE: 1:1-4 The historical reality of the Christian message

Summary: First John, like the Gospel, begins with a prologue. The entire emphasis is upon the historical reality of what our author and his fellow Christians have experienced. This is the word of life (v. 1), the message that

105

PROLOGUE

1 ¹This is what we proclaim to you:
what was from the beginning,
what we have heard,
what we have seen with our eyes,
what we have looked upon
and our hands have touched—
we speak of the word of life.
²(This life became visible;
we have seen and bear witness to it,
and we proclaim to you the eternal life
that was present to the Father
and became visible to us.)

³What we have seen and heard
we proclaim in turn to you
so that you may share life with us.
This fellowship of ours is with the
Father
and with his Son, Jesus Christ.
⁴Indeed, our purpose in writing you this
is that our joy may be complete.

The Light of God

⁵Here, then, is the message
we have heard from him
and announce to you:

has been heard and is now to be proclaimed. The message, however, has been incarnated in a human being, the Son, Jesus Christ (v. 3), who was actually heard and seen and touched. In him eternal life became visible so that both he and it might be shared with us (vv. 2-3). This is a fellowship (*koinōnia*) with both Father and Son, and the very act of describing it in writing is, for the author, a source of consummate joy (v. 4).

Comments: This short section is not written with smooth articulation — thus the breaks in continuity, usually indicated in English translations by a dash or parentheses or both. It is almost as though the author were speaking extemporaneously, with the natural breaks in thought that occur away from the discipline of pen and ink. Notable are the phrases reminiscent of the Fourth Gospel, though their content has slight differences from the Gospel meaning. The "from the beginning" of verse 1 is not a reference to eternity (John 1:1), but to the inception of the gospel preaching. The "word of life" (v. 1) is not exclusively that word which became flesh (John 1:14), but the *gospel message* that became audible, visible, and tangible in the human Jesus.

Does the insistence upon hearing, seeing, and touching demand that the author be an eyewitness to the words and works of the historical Jesus? That, surely, is the most obvious meaning. Yet the words also permit the solid possibility that the author is simply, but forcefully, uniting himself to the actual eyewitnesses from whom he has derived his version of the good news. Through them — and he can summon them up in his memory — he has truly experienced the Lord and his word of life.

1:5-2:2 Walking in the light: the question of sin

Summary: Part of the message for Christians is that there is a sphere of life and righteousness that can be called "light." It is God's sphere, for "God

that God is light;
in him there is no darkness.

Claims of False Teachers

[6]If we say, "We have fellowship with
him,"
while continuing to walk in darkness,
we are liars and do not act in truth.
[7]But if we walk in light,
as he is in the light,
we have fellowship with one another,
and the blood of his Son Jesus cleanses
us from all sin.
[8]If we say, "We are free of the guilt of
sin,"
we deceive ourselves; the truth is not
to be found in us.

[9]But if we acknowledge our sins,
he who is just can be trusted
to forgive our sins
and cleanse us from every wrong.
[10]If we say, "We have never sinned,"
we make him a liar
and his word finds no place in us.

2 [1]My little ones,
I am writing this to keep you from
sin.
But if anyone should sin,
we have, in the presence of the Father,
Jesus Christ, an intercessor who is
just.
[2]He is an offering for our sins,
and not for our sins only,
but for those of the whole world.

is light" (v. 5). But there is another sphere, too, which is that of darkness, of untruth, and there are those who walk in it. To have fellowship with both God (v. 6) and one another (v. 7), we must walk in the light, cleansed from sin by the blood of God's Son (v. 7). This cleansing demands from us a personal acknowledgement of our sin, which will be answered by the cleansing that comes from God. To pretend that we have never sinned is, in itself, a lie that would continue to bind us to the sphere of darkness (vv. 8-10). Such admission of sin is by no means a suggestion that sin makes little difference in Christian life. Our author's purpose in writing is to keep Christians from sin (2:1). Yet, though living in the light, he is not blinded by it: he can see that Christians can and, on occasions, still do sin. Christ, however, remains effective, both as intercessor (Paraclete) and as sin-offering, and not for us only but for the whole world (2:1-2).

Comments: There are a number of peculiarities in this section. "God is light," says verse 5, a statement that is not too strange after our study of the Fourth Gospel, but yet is a bit different. In the Gospel the emphasis falls on *Jesus* as the light of the world (John 8:12; 9:5).

A second peculiarity is the description of Jesus as a sin-offering (2:2) whose blood not only cleanses *us* from all sin (v. 7) but is effective for the whole world (2:2). This, too, is an emphasis not seen in the Fourth Gospel, for which Jesus' death is not nearly so much expiatory—perhaps only and barely in the Lamb of God statement (John 1:29)—as revelatory of God's love.

The "little ones" of 2:1 is a third novelty. In John's Gospel the author's posture is egalitarian: the followers of Christ are simply disciples (*mathētai*),

Keeping the Commandments

[3]The way we can be sure of our knowledge of him
is to keep his commandments.
[4]The man who claims, "I have known him,"
without keeping his commandments,
is a liar; in such a one there is no truth.
[5]But whoever keeps his word,
truly has the love of God been made perfect in him.
The way we can be sure we are in union with him
[6]is for the man who claims to abide in him
to conduct himself just as he did.
[7]Dearly beloved,
it is no new commandment that I write to you,
but an old one which you had from the start.
The commandment, now old, is the word you have already heard.

[8]On second thought, the commandment that I write you is new,
as it is realized in him and you,
for the darkness is over
and the real light begins to shine.
[9]The man who claims to be in light,
hating his brother all the while,
is in darkness even now.
[10]The man who continues in the light
is the one who loves his brother;
there is nothing in him to cause a fall.
[11]But the man who hates his brother is in darkness.
He walks in shadows,
not knowing where he is going,
since the dark has blinded his eyes.

Members of the Community

[12]Little ones, I address you,
for through his Name your sins have been forgiven.
[13]Fathers, I address you,
for you have known him who is from the beginning.

and there is little, if any, hierarchy evident. First John makes extensive use of "little ones" and, in so doing, gives a picture of a person of special responsibility addressing Christians whom he fully expects to listen to his advice and pleading.

Finally, it comes as a surprise for those reading 2:2 in the Greek, or from a literal translation, to find Jesus called "Paraclete" (intercessor). John's Gospel reserves that name for the Spirit, though John 14:16 does call the Spirit "another Paraclete," thus leaving room for Jesus, too, to fulfill that function.

2:3-17 Keeping the commandments

Summary: Christianity is not simply a "head trip," a question only of knowledge. It demands a life consonant with the God of love we claim to know and experience. Fortunately, we have a human exemplar to follow and thus are challenged (v. 6) to conduct ourselves just as Jesus did.

And this means a challenge to love (vv. 7-11). In a sense, this is now an old commandment, one that Christians have heard from the beginning of their instruction (v. 7). On the other hand, it is still new, for Jesus has given us the abiding newness of his own example, which we renew in ourselves (v. 8). We must live in one of two polarities: in the light that is the sphere of

Young men, I address you,
for you have conquered the evil one.
¹⁴I address you, children,
for you have known the Father.
I address you, fathers,
for you have known him who is from
the beginning.
I address you, young men,
for you are strong,
and the word of God remains in you,
and you have conquered the evil one.

Against the World

¹⁵Have no love for the world,
nor the things that the world affords.
If anyone loves the world,
the Father's love has no place in him,
¹⁶for nothing that the world affords
comes from the Father.
Carnal allurements,
enticements for the eye,
the life of empty show—
all these are from the world.

reciprocal love (v. 10) or in the darkness of hatred (v. 11), where one can only stumble blindly in darkness (vv. 9, 11).

Encouragement flows out to the inhabitants of the light: to the "little ones . . . the children" (vv. 12, 14), who, though spiritually immature, have, through personal experience of the Father, been freed from sin; to the "fathers" (vv. 13-14), the spiritually mature, whose knowledge of the Father is secure and unmovable; to the "young men" (vv. 13-14), the spiritually proficient, whose strength, rising from the abiding word of God, has conquered the evil one.

All of these Christians are now advised to treat the ungodly world with cautious discernment (vv. 15-17). Passions, greed, wealth and its trappings (v. 16) leave no place for the Father's love to dwell (v. 15). Whereas all things are transitory, the one who does God's will abides forever (v. 17).

Comments: The material in this section has a loose unity, held together by the obedience to the commandments of the initial verses (3-8) and by the doing of God's will (an identical concept) in the final verse (17). The emphasis throughout falls on love. It would be possible to interpret "just as he did" (v. 6) of God the Father, but this expression is uniformly used in 1 John of Jesus. Our author has no difficulty in passing imperceptibly from the Father to the Son, as he does here.

The precise meaning of "little ones . . . children," "fathers," "young men" of verses 12-14 is much disputed. The designations could refer to age groups. Or the "fathers . . . young men" could be officials (like presbyters and deacons) in the community, the membership of which would be referred to in general as the "little ones." We suggest that these names loosely differentiate states of spiritual maturity. Emphasis—by final position and length of description—falls on the "young men," those advanced in spirituality yet not completely mature, who bear the brunt of the crisis that has occasioned this writing. No one explanation of this terminology has been accepted by all scholars.

¹⁷And the world with its seductions is
   passing away
but the man who does God's will
   endures forever.

Against Antichrists

¹⁸Children, it is the final hour;
just as you heard that the antichrist
   was coming,
so now many such antichrists have appeared.
This makes us certain that it is the final
   hour.
¹⁹It was from our ranks that they took
   their leave —
not that they really belonged to us;
for if they had belonged to us,

they would have stayed with us.
It only served to show that none of
   them was ours.
²⁰But you have the anointing that comes
   from the Holy One,
so that all knowledge is yours.
²¹My reason for having written you
is not that you do not know the truth
but that you do,
and that no lie has anything in common
   with the truth.
²²Who is the liar?
He who denies that Jesus is the Christ.
He is the antichrist,
denying the Father and the Son.
²³Anyone who denies the Son
has no claim on the Father,

Verses 15-17 are surely a pessimistic summation of Christian relationship to the world. As was true in the Gospel, this is largely a question of language. The world of which these verses speak is not God's world, not the "whole world" for which Jesus is an offering for sin (2:2), but the sphere of anti-God, that is, of unlove and untruth. It will be personified in the antichrists of the following verses.

2:18-27 Warning against false teachers, the antichrists

Summary: The appearance of antichrists tolls the final hour (v. 18). Sad to report, they come "from our ranks" (v. 19), and it is they who now "try to deceive you" (v. 26). Protection comes from the divine anointing that provides knowledge (v. 20), that teaches all truth, so that, free from any lie, "you have no need for anyone to teach you" (v. 27).

Comments: The "final hour" (v. 18) is a common motif throughout the other New Testament writings, though certainly not central to the theology of John's Gospel, where Jesus' future coming is very secondary to his already experienced presence. The term "antichrists" is found only in this epistle and 2 John among the whole of the New Testament literature. It is similar, however, to the "false christs" of Mark 13:22 — they, too, are signs of an impending judgment. Cardinal John Henry Newman suggested that the movement of salvation history went along on a straight line up to the brink of the end time, where it changed direction ninety degrees to follow along on the edge of the precipice. Our Christian lives, in this description, would be lived on the brink, just a step away from the plunge into the beyond.

but he who acknowledges the Son
can claim the Father as well.

Life for God's Anointed

²⁴As for you,
let what you heard from the beginning
remain in your hearts.
If what you heard from the beginning
does remain in your hearts,
then you in turn will remain in the Son
and in the Father.
²⁵He himself made us a promise
and the promise is no less than this:
eternal life.
²⁶I have written you these things
about those who try to deceive you.

²⁷As for you,
the anointing you received from him
remains in your hearts.
This means you have no need
for anyone to teach you.
Rather, as his anointing teaches you
about all things
and is true — free from any lie —
remain in him
as that anointing taught you.

Children of God

²⁸Remain in him now, little ones,
so that, when he reveals himself,
we may be fully confident
and not retreat in shame at his coming.

Verse 19 indicates the crisis that has occasioned this epistle. Members have left the Johannine community, members whose very exit proved their insincerity. Like Judas (John 13:30), whom our author may consider as their model, they went out into the darkness. The insistence on knowledge and truth apparent in the following verses (20-27) makes it evident that those who left were faulty in their teaching. Verse 22 is to the point: "Who is the liar? He who denies that Jesus is the Christ. He is the antichrist, denying the Father and the Son." This appears to be an out-and-out denial that Jesus was the Christ, a denial, then, of the central theology of John's Gospel: ". . . to help you believe that Jesus is the Messiah, the Son of God, so that through this faith you may have life in his name" (20:31). Further passages in 1 John will give us more evidence about the content of this disbelief. The accent in this passage is on faith.

Defense against errant teaching will be provided by the divine anointing (vv. 20, 27) that we have all received, our Christing ("anointing" is *chrisma* in Greek) in baptism with the teaching (vv. 20, 27) provided at that time (v. 24) and our subsequent dwelling in both the Son and the Father (v. 24). This is eternal life, and the promise of an even greater sharing in it (v. 25).

2:28–3:24 Children of God, children of the devil, love versus hatred

Summary: If we but remain in God, our future is without fear, since the holiness of our lives will prove that we are God's children (2:28-29). And indeed, this is precisely what we are now by God's love (v. 1). And we shall become even more intimate children as, seeing him as he is, we meld into his likeness (v. 2). If only we remain pure as he is (v. 3), holy as the Son is holy (v. 7).

²⁹If you consider the holiness that is his,
you can be sure that everyone who acts
in holiness
has been begotten by him.

3 ¹See what love the Father has be-
stowed on us
in letting us be called children of God!
Yet that is what we are.
The reason the world does not recognize us
is that it never recognized the Son.
²Dearly beloved,
we are God's children now;
what we shall later be has not yet come
to light.
We know that when it comes to light
we shall be like him,
for we shall see him as he is.
³Everyone who has this hope based on
him
keeps himself pure, as he is pure.

Avoiding Sin

⁴Everyone who sins acts lawlessly
for sin is lawlessness.
⁵You know well that the reason he revealed himself
was to take away sins;
in him there is nothing sinful.
⁶The man who remains in him does not
sin.
The man who sins has not seen him
or known him.
⁷Little ones,
let no one deceive you;
the man who acts in holiness is holy
indeed,
even as the Son is holy.
⁸The man who sins belongs to the devil,
because the devil is a sinner from the
beginning.
It was to destroy the devil's works
that the Son of God revealed himself.
⁹No one begotten of God acts sinfully
because he remains of God's stock;
he cannot sin
because he is begotten of God.
¹⁰That is the way to see who are God's
children,
and who are the devil's.
No one whose actions are unholy belongs to God,
nor anyone who fails to love his
brother.

The other option is to exist and act in the sphere of sin and lawlessness
(v. 4), which is to become a child of the devil, one whose actions are unholy, specifically one who does not love (v. 10).

That we love one another was our first instruction (v. 11), and in this
love we have passed from death to life (v. 14). The opposite is to become the
devil's child like Cain (Gen 4), who killed his brother in jealous rage, just as
the anti-God world now rages against us (v. 13). Not to love is death, the
condition of both the murderer and the hater (vv. 14-15). Our call, on the
contrary, is to lay down our lives for one another as Christ sacrificed his for
us (v. 16). This means, at least, to share what we have with the needy (vv.
17-18). If we do, even though we may be imperfect (v. 20), the magnani-
mous God will be with us (vv. 20-21), and with him, his peace (v. 19). But
all depends on this double commandment: that we *believe* in his Son, Jesus
Christ, and *love* one another (v. 23). If we do, God remains in us, evident
by his gift of the Spirit (v. 24).

Comments: Verse 2:28 speaks again of Jesus' coming, the final hour of
2:18. As we noted, this is a minor issue in John's Gospel.

Keeping the Commandments

¹¹This, remember, is the message
you heard from the beginning:
we should love one another.
¹²We should not follow the example of
Cain
who belonged to the evil one
and killed his brother.
Why did he kill him?
Because his own deeds were wicked
while his brother's were just.
¹³No need, then, brothers, to be surprised
if the world hates you.
¹⁴That we have passed from death to life
we know
because we love the brothers.
The man who does not love is among
the living dead.
¹⁵Anyone who hates his brother is a
murderer,
and you know that eternal life
abides in no murderer's heart.

¹⁶The way we came to understand love
was that he laid down his life for us;
we too must lay down our lives for our
brothers.
¹⁷I ask you, how can God's love sur-
vive in a man
who has enough of this world's goods
yet closes his heart to his brother
when he sees him in need?
¹⁸Little children,
let us love in deed and in truth
and not merely talk about it.
¹⁹This is our way of knowing we are
committed to the truth
and are at peace before him
²⁰no matter what our consciences may
charge us with;
for God is greater than our hearts
and all is known to him.
²¹Beloved,
if our consciences have nothing to
charge us with,
we can be sure that God is with us

The repeated reference to the "children of God" (vv. 1, 2, 10) employs the language and distinction of the Gospel. Christians are God's children, the *tekna Theou;* only Jesus is God's Son, the *huios Theou.* As our author describes the "begotten of God" (v. 9), he slips into strongly figurative language. The Greek of verse 9 speaks of God's seed remaining in his children. John 3:1 has already insisted that this is what we really are — God's children!

The imagery of verse 2 is fascinating. Looking at God as though into a mirror, our own visage is reflected, but with divine configuration. As God's children we will, says the author, bear an amazing family likeness.

Verse 3 is ambiguous. Are we to keep ourselves pure as God is pure or as Jesus is pure? Probably the latter, since in subsequent verses it is Christ who is sinless (v. 5) and the Son who is holy (v. 7).

Verse 4 seems simplistic in stating that sin is lawlessness, but our author wants to insist that there are definitely things that we *should do* and others that we *should not do.* Disobedience is sin, the pattern of the devil (v. 8), who from the beginning fostered disobedience unto death (Gen 3:4-5). John 8:44 concludes in a similar fashion that the devil was a liar and murderer from the beginning. His followers are his children (John 8:44), and for 1 John the murderer Cain is an example (v. 12).

²²and that we will receive at his hands whatever we ask.
Why? Because we are keeping his commandments
and doing what is pleasing in his sight.
²³His commandment is this:
we are to believe in the name of his Son, Jesus Christ,
and are to love one another as he commanded us.
²⁴Those who keep his commandments remain in him
and he in them.
And this is how we know that he remains in us:
from the Spirit that he gave us.

Testing the Spirits

4 ¹Beloved,
do not trust every spirit,
but put the spirits to a test
to see if they belong to God,
because many false prophets have appeared in the world.
²This is how you can recognize God's Spirit:
every spirit that acknowledges Jesus Christ come in the flesh
belongs to God,
³while every spirit that fails to acknowledge him
does not belong to God.
Such is the spirit of the antichrist

The double reference to the laying down of life in verse 16 recalls the repeated statement in John 10:11-18 that Jesus, as good shepherd, would lay down his life for his sheep.

Verse 23 provides in miniature the theological heart of 1 John: we must *believe* in God's Son, Jesus the Christ, and *love* one another. Belief and love — basically 1 John speaks of nothing else. Where these obtain, the divine indwelling is an accomplished fact, to which the presence of the Spirit testifies. This first mention of the Spirit in 1 John leads us into the following section.

4:1-6 The two spirits

Summary: Be not immediately impressed by a powerful spiritual presence, however, for it may indicate the spirit of antichrist (v. 3), that of the many false prophets who have gone out (from us) into the world (v. 1). The spirits must be tested, and the test is crucial: Do they, or do they not, believe that Jesus Christ has come in the flesh? (v. 2). It is this which we believe and by which we, with the strength of God, have won the victory (v. 4). Those who do not believe belong to the anti-God world that listens to them (v. 5). Theirs is the spirit of deception, ours the spirit of truth (v. 6).

Comments: This question of discernment of spirits comes down to a single practical test: What do the prophets — true or false — believe? What do they teach about Jesus? If they acknowledge Jesus Christ come in the flesh, they are genuine Christians; if they do not, they are false prophets and belong to the world. This test is a clarification of the doctrinal difficulty first expressed in 2:22: "Who is the liar? He who denies that Jesus is the Christ." The faith statement "Jesus is the Christ" is nuanced now in verse 2 to insist

which, as you have heard, is to come;
in fact, it is in the world already.
⁴You are of God, you little ones,
and thus you have conquered the false
   prophets.
For there is One greater in you
than there is in the world.
⁵Those others belong to the world;
that is why theirs is the language of the
   world
and why the world listens to them.
⁶We belong to God
and anyone who has knowledge of
   God gives us a hearing,
while anyone who is not of God refuses to hear us.
Thus do we distinguish the spirit of
   truth
from the spirit of deception.

God's Love and Ours

⁷Beloved,
let us love one another

because love is of God;
everyone who loves is begotten of God
and has knowledge of God.
⁸The man without love has known
   nothing of God,
for God is love.
⁹God's love was revealed in our midst
   in this way:
he sent his only Son to the world
that we might have life through him.
¹⁰Love, then, consists in this:
not that we have loved God
but that he has loved us
and has sent his Son as an offering for
   our sins.
¹¹Beloved,
if God has loved us so,
we must have the same love for one
   another.
¹²No one has ever seen God.
Yet if we love one another
God dwells in us,

that "Jesus Christ has come in the flesh." *The emphasis falls on the humanity of Jesus.* He in whom we believe, he whose name we bear as Christians, is Son of God, is the Christ, is intimately united with the Father, and is also, and of his essence, *a human being.* It is about this last phrase that the controversy rages, a controversy that, for the author, is absolutely critical for Christian faith.

That the world listens to the opponents (v. 5), to the false prophets (v. 1) with the spirit of antichrist (v. 3), indicates that the opposition is having considerable success. Is our author's group in danger of becoming a minority among what had been a united Johannine community?

4:7-21 God's love inspires ours

Summary: God is love (vv. 8, 16), and he has first loved us (vv. 10, 16, 19). He evidenced this love through the gift of his Son (v. 9), sent as Savior (v. 14). Because God has so loved us, we too must become lovers (v. 9), lovers of one another (vv. 7, 11, 12, 20, 21). Only if we love the visible neighbor can we love the invisible God (vv. 12, 20).

God's love for us and our love for him and for one another should afford us fearless confidence (v. 18), for we have overcome the world just as Christ has (v. 17). It is in him as Savior of the world and as Son of God that we profess our faith through the Spirit (vv. 13-14). On the other hand, sadly

and his love is brought to perfection in us.
¹³The way we know we remain in him and he in us
is that he has given us of his Spirit.
¹⁴We have seen for ourselves, and can testify,
that the Father has sent the Son as savior of the world.
¹⁵When anyone acknowledges that Jesus is the Son of God,
God dwells in him
and he in God.
¹⁶We have come to know and to believe in the love God has for us.
God is love,
and he who abides in love
abides in God,
and God in him.
¹⁷Our love is brought to perfection in this,
that we should have confidence on the day of judgment;
for our relation to this world is just like his.
¹⁸Love has no room for fear;
rather, perfect love casts out all fear.
And since fear has to do with punishment,
love is not yet perfect in one who is afraid.
¹⁹We, for our part, love
because he first loved us.
²⁰If anyone says, "My love is fixed on God,"
yet hates his brother,
he is a liar.
One who has no love for the brother he has seen
cannot love the God he has not seen.
²¹The commandment we have from him is this:

and simply, the man without love has known nothing of God (v. 8); his profession of love for God without love for neighbor is a disastrous lie (v. 20).

Comments: This section is a tight unity concentrating without distraction on the one point that God's love generates ours. The verses are linked together by numerous connections: 8//16; 10//16//19; 10//14; 12//20; 20//21, with the whole converging on the central truth that if God has loved us we must have similar love for one another (v. 11). That "God is love" (vv. 8, 16) is now the second description of God given in this epistle; we have already seen that "God is light" (1:5). God is not love in the abstract but in all his activity. He creates lovingly, he saves lovingly, he judges lovingly. Our God is a God of love.

Reference to the Spirit (v. 13) returns us for a moment to the context of 4:1-6. It is the Spirit, as in 4:2, who enables us to affirm the truth — the truth that Jesus is Savior of the world, that he is Son of God (4:14-15). The basic creedal affirmations of this Johannine community are assuming a more definite shape. For the Johannine Christian, Jesus is the Christ (2:22) come in the flesh (4:2); Jesus is Savior (3:16; 4:14), an offering for the sins of the world (1:7; 2:2; 4:10); Jesus is Son of God (3:23; 4:15).

5:1-13 Faith: conclusion

Summary: All who believe that Jesus is the Christ (v. 1), the Son of God (v. 5), are themselves children of God, to be loved as is their Father (v. 1). In

whoever loves God must also love his brother.

5 ¹Everyone who believes that Jesus is the Christ
has been begotten of God.
Now, everyone who loves the father
loves the child he has begotten.
²We can be sure that we love God's children
when we love God
and do what he has commanded.
³The love of God consists in this:
that we keep his commandments —
and his commandments are not burdensome.
⁴Everyone begotten of God conquers the world,
and the power that has conquered the world
is this faith of ours.
⁵Who, then, is conqueror of the world?
The one who believes that Jesus is the Son of God.
⁶Jesus Christ it is who came through water and blood —
not in water only,
but in water and in blood.
It is the Spirit who testifies to this,
and the Spirit is truth.
⁷Thus there are three that testify,
⁸the Spirit and the water and the blood —
and these three are of one accord.
⁹Do we not accept human testimony?
The testimony of God is much greater:
it is the testimony God has given
on his own Son's behalf.
¹⁰Whoever believes in the Son of God
possesses that testimony within his heart.
Whoever does not believe God
has made God a liar

fact, this reciprocal love is the Father's unburdensome command (v. 3), originating from the Christian faith that has conquered the world (vv. 4-5).

Faith is belief in Jesus Christ, who came in essential humanity, in a human ministry stretching from baptism till human death, both testified to by the Spirit (v. 6). Not only does the Spirit testify, but so too do the present-day water and blood (v. 8) — the sacraments of baptism and Eucharist — which bespeak the presence of Christ himself and the eternal life he brings (vv. 11-12). Spirit, water, and blood are part of God's testimony. To deny them is to reject God's own witness and to affirm that he is a liar (v. 10). And, indeed, the purpose of this whole epistle is to help all to realize that they actually possess eternal life — if, that is, they believe in the Son of God (v. 13).

Comments: To the preceding section on love (4:7-21), recalled briefly in 5:1-3, is now added a section on faith. The creedal statement proposed here is that Jesus is the Son of God (vv. 5, 10, 12) — but a Son of God who is also thoroughly human, both at the baptism (at which the Spirit testified in John 1:33-34) that initiated the ministry and in the bloody death that terminated it. Son of God, yes — but a Son of God whose humanity was essential. This is the insistence of verse 6. In verses 7-8 a shift is made. To the Spirit as witness are added both the water and blood. The historical incidents of verse 6 are replaced by the sacraments. The Spirit still testifies to Jesus, and

117

by refusing to believe in the testimony he has given on his own Son's behalf. ¹¹The testimony is this:

God gave us eternal life,
and this life is in his Son.
¹²Whoever possesses the Son
possesses life;
whoever does not possess the Son of
God
does not possess life.

¹³I have written this to you to make you realize that you possess eternal life —you who believe in the name of the Son of God.

Prayer for Sinners. ¹⁴We have this confidence in God: that he hears us whenever we ask for anything according to his will. ¹⁵And since we know that he hears us whenever we ask, we know that what we have asked him for is ours. ¹⁶Anyone who sees his brother sinning, if the sin is not deadly, should petition God, and thus life will be given to the sinner. This is only for those whose sin is not deadly. There is such a thing as a deadly sin; I do not say that one should pray about that. ¹⁷True, all wrongdoing is sin, but not all sin is deadly.

so do the sacraments of baptism and Eucharist. All three give their testimony in the Christian assembly: the Spirit through those speakers who are his inspired mouthpiece; baptism and Eucharist as signs of the eternal life that God gives us in his Son (vv. 11-12), as occasions during which faith in Jesus is solemnly affirmed and strengthened.

Verse 13 looks very much like a conclusion and, indeed, bears striking resemblance to John 20:31, the original conclusion to the Fourth Gospel. Apparently to this conclusion to the epistle have been added the final verses, 14-21.

5:14-21 Prayer for sinners, summary

Summary: Our prayer should be made in complete confidence: what we ask for is already ours (vv. 14-15). One specific thing we should request is the conversion of the sinner, except in the case of one sinning in deadly fashion—there is doubt about that (vv. 16-17). We who are begotten by God, however, will not sin, shielded as we are by Christ, part of God's sphere and not of the devil's, to whom belongs the anti-God world (vv. 18-19). Actually we indwell both the Father and the Son, true God and eternal life. One final word—guard yourselves from the idols.

Comments: This short section touches on four different points. The first (vv. 14-15) is simple: Ask and you shall receive (Matt 7:7-8; Luke 11:9-10). God's door is always open. The second (vv. 16-17) is considerably more complicated. We are encouraged to pray for Christian sinners with the promise that this prayer, too, will be answered. But the author expresses serious doubt about the value and efficacy of prayer for those Christians sinning in deadly fashion. He does not say not to pray for them, but he hesitates to encourage it: "I do not say that one should pray about that" (v. 16). He must view those whose sin is deadly as ex-Christians who have, with

¹⁸We know that no one begotten of God commits sin; rather, God protects the one begotten by him, and so the evil one cannot touch him. ¹⁹We know that we belong to God, while the whole world is under the evil one. ²⁰We know, too, that the Son of God has come and has given us discernment to recognize the One who is true. And we are in the One who is true, for we are in his Son Jesus Christ. He is the true God and eternal life.

²¹My little children, be on your guard against idols.

---

fatal deliberation, moved out into the darkness. Unfortunately for us readers, the deadly sin is not described. Some commentators have suggested murder and adultery, but it seems more in accord with the whole of 1 John to identify the sin as deliberate apostasy — the choice of darkness over light, of death over life, of hatred over love.

The third point (vv. 18-20) presents a rather black-and-white world view. On the one side are ranged the children of God, protected by divine power, dwelling in both Father and Son, graced by divine life; on the other side are the evil one and his anti-God world. For twentieth-century readers the contrast is too strong, too definite. The modern world in which we live specializes in shadows.

The epistle concludes with a terse warning against the idols. These are, in all probability, not false images but false doctrines, especially those that peek out between the lines of this letter — a faulty appreciation of Jesus' humanity and of its saving power.

CONCLUSIONS TO OUR STUDY OF 1 JOHN

This first, and principal, of the three Johannine epistles is elusive. It says nothing about its author, little about his community and about the crisis that occasioned the writing of this epistle. Even the doctrinal elements lack sharp definition. Yet some conclusions can be drawn regarding all of these elements.

1. Occasion. The clearest evidence can be found in 2:19, where we are told that the opponents, the "antichrists," are people who *exited from the author's own community.* They are described as deceivers (2:26) against whom the epistle hopes that the Spirit and instruction received in baptism will provide protection (2:20, 24-27). They are false prophets (4:1) whose spirit is one of deception (4:6). It is their teaching, surely, that constitutes the idols, the false doctrines, of the epistle's final verse. The author has clearly been shocked and offended by this terrible split in the community. He hesitates even to hope that something can be done to repair it (5:16). Whereas the Johannine community of the Gospel has been excommunicated from the synagogue, the community of 1 John has been abandoned by

119

Christians (1 John would hardly call them that) who no longer wish to share belief and life.

2. Theology. (a) The nature and work of *Jesus Christ* is the central issue. The epistle insists, as we have seen, that Jesus is the Christ (2:22; 5:1), come in the flesh (4:2); that Jesus is Savior (3:16; 4:14), an offering for the sins of the world (1:7; 2:2; 4:10); that Jesus is the Son of God (3:23; 4:15; 5:5, 10, 11-13); that Jesus came through both water and blood (5:6). Although these elements still do not allow us to paint a completely clear picture of what 1 John is arguing for and against, it must be that the opponents are challenging Jesus' humanity and its salvific function. A little later in the history of the church, Cerinthus would teach that the supernatural Christ descended upon the man Jesus at baptism, revealing God during Jesus' ministry, and departed from Jesus before his death. This presented an antiseptic Christ, hardly touched by Jesus' humanity, and not touched at all by his death. If the opponents of 1 John have not quite arrived at the position of Cerinthus, they are well on the way. For them Jesus' humanity was not of salvific importance. And so 1 John insists on the flesh, on the death, on the salvific function, on the offering for the sins of the world. For 1 John, Jesus — the man Jesus — was truly Son of God, but in this unique Sonship the truth and value of his humanity were never diminished. This same insistence on Jesus' humanity may explain why 1 John is considerably more God-centered than the Fourth Gospel. The more emphasis placed on Jesus come in the flesh, the sharper the contrast between him and the eternal Father.

b) The epistle's *moral teaching* is almost too simple. Two verbs describe it all: *believe* and *love*. The author is anguished by those whose belief has been corrupted, by those whose love stands denounced by the very fact of their departure. And so the epistle insists that we believe what was taught from the beginning (1:1; 2:7, 24; 3:11) and that we can only love God if we unfailingly love one another. The core of 1 John's ethics is given clearly in 3:23: "We are to believe in the name of his Son, Jesus Christ, and are to love one another."

c) The position of the *Paraclete* in 1 John is subdued in comparison to the importance of this figure in the Fourth Gospel. Actually, the word occurs only once, in 1 John 2:1, where, surprisingly, it is applied to Jesus, who intercedes for us in the presence of his Father. The entire function of the Spirit gets only brief attention. The references to the anointing in 2:20-27 may refer to the Spirit, but without specification, and the first clear reference is in 3:24, which leads immediately into a warning about testing the spirits (4:1-6). We find other references to the Spirit only in 4:13 and 5:6-7. A scholarly guess is that the opponents have argued so strongly from the supposed presence of the Spirit in bolstering their own positions that the author of 1 John has backed off a bit from a strong Paraclete theology, lest he play into their hands.

3. Author and community. The epistle leaves its author unnamed, without even references such as those to the Beloved Disciple that indicate either authorship or original testimony in the Fourth Gospel. The epistle resembles the Gospel in vocabulary and in theological emphases, though these latter show nuanced differences from those of the Gospel. The epistle also seems to be from a later period when the opponents are no longer outsiders, as in the Fourth Gospel, but fellow Christians who have broken unity with the group. These characteristics point with some firmness to a writer different from the evangelist but thoroughly imbued with his theology, writing some years — not necessarily many — after the Gospel was published. About A.D. 100 is a good guess. Some scholars believe that he may have been the writer who re-edited the Gospel by adding on material such as chapter 21. That is possible but not certain, though 3 John 12 must be editorially related to John 21:24. His community is Johannine, related closely in mentality to the Fourth Gospel, with a theology differing from, but not contradictory to, that of the other Gospels. It is a community with little evidence of structured authority, more egalitarian than hierarchical. And it is a community which, perhaps because of that very non-hierarchical structure, has suffered a devastating schism. Unity has been broken. Our author has taken up pen and ink to encourage faithfulness, to protect the truth, to inspire mutual love.

The Second Epistle of John

Text and Commentary

¹The elder to a Lady who is elect and to her children.

In truth I love each of you—and not only I but also all those who have come to know the truth. ²This love is based on the truth that abides in us and will be with us forever. ³In truth and love, then, we shall have grace, mercy, and peace from God the Father and from Jesus Christ, the Father's Son.

⁴It has given me great joy to find some of your children walking in the path of truth, just as we were commanded by the Father. ⁵But now, my Lady, I would make this request of you (not as if I were writing you some new commandment; rather, it is a commandment we have had from the start): let us love one another. ⁶This love involves our walking according to the commandments, and as you have heard from the beginning, the commandment is the way in which you should walk.

⁷Many deceitful men have gone out into the world, men who do not acknowledge Jesus Christ as coming in the flesh. Such is the deceitful one! This is the antichrist! ⁸Look out that you yourselves do not lose what you have worked for; you must receive your reward in full. ⁹Anyone who is so "progressive" that he does not remain rooted in the teaching of Christ does not possess God, while anyone who remains rooted in the teaching possesses both the Father and the Son. ¹⁰If anyone comes to you who does not bring this teaching, do not receive him into your house; do not even greet him, ¹¹for whoever greets him shares in the evil he does.

¹²While there is much more that I could write you, I do not intend to put it down on paper; instead, I hope to visit you and talk with you face to face, so that our joy may be full.

¹³The children of your elect sister send you their greetings.

(Before studying what follows, please read and reread, slowly and aloud, the Second Epistle of John itself.)

Structure: The Second Epistle of John is a short letter, just long enough to fill one papyrus sheet. It contains the ordinary letter divisions of the time: the introduction (vv. 1-3); the note of happiness or thanksgiving (v. 4); the body of the letter (vv. 5-11); the conclusion (vv. 12-13).

Occasion and contents: The letter fits well into the picture of the Johannine community sketched out at the end of 1 John. Visitors to the author, who now terms himself "the elder" (v. 1), have shown themselves faithful to the truth as he sees it (v. 4). So he writes with joy to the Johannine church (the "lady" of vv. 1, 5) from which they have come to express his happiness and to tender his advice. The advice, not surprisingly, concerns *love* and

122

belief. They are to love one another (vv. 5-6). Equally, they must beware of those who have broken unity, the antichrists who deny that Jesus Christ has come in the flesh (vv. 7-9). They should not even offer them welcome, lest their homes become the pulpits of the evil one (vv. 10-11).

The note concludes with hope for an impending visit and greetings from the members of the author's own church, the children of their elect sister (v. 13).

1 and 2 John were most probably authored by the same person who in 2 John warns a different Johannine community of the dangers spelled out at length in the first epistle. The two epistles are, consequently, closely related, written because of the same crisis, by the same author, and most probably about the same time, close to A.D. 100.

Comments: (a) Verses 1 and 13, the beginning and the end, use identical terminology. The letter is addressed to the *elect* lady and her *children* and encloses final greetings from the *children* of her *elect* sister. It is ecclesiastical language that is being used. The elect lady and her elect sister are sister churches, of which the children are the members. The "elder" of verse 1 is an ambiguous term. It means more than "older man," since the author calls himself "*the* elder" and addresses the church with some degree of authority. The most probable meaning of the designation is that the author is a second-generation Christian who has known the eyewitnesses of primitive Christianity and can, therefore, testify to what was seen and taught from the beginning.

b) The Johannine polarity between believers and deceivers is strongly phrased. There are those who know the truth, in whom it abides, and who walk in the truth with love (vv. 1-6). And there are the others, antichrists, who do not confess Jesus Christ coming in the flesh (v. 7). The theological framework is clearly that of 1 John. Verse 9 has an interesting phrase that would be rendered literally: "Everyone *going ahead* and not remaining in the truth . . . ." Our own jargon might term them radical "progressives" who abandoned the traditional truth for novelty. Certainly that is the way 2 John views them. The author has a real fear, reflected in verse 8, that his sister Johannine community might succumb to such novelty. It is that fear which moves him to bar house churches and their pulpits to such prophets of false doctrine (vv. 10-11).

c) Verse 12 is an affirmation that personal encounter is of more value than literary correspondence.

The Third Epistle of John

Text and Commentary

¹The elder to the beloved Gaius, whom indeed I love.

²Beloved, I hope you are in good health — may you thrive in all other ways as you do in the spirit. ³For it has given me great joy to have the brothers bear witness to how truly you walk in the path of truth. ⁴Nothing delights me more than to hear that my children are walking in this path.

⁵Beloved, you demonstrate fidelity by all that you do for the brothers even though they are strangers; ⁶indeed, they have testified to your love before the church. And you will do a good thing if, in a way that pleases God, you help them to continue their journey. ⁷It was for the sake of the Name that they set out, and they are accepting nothing from the pagans. ⁸Therefore, we owe it to such men to support them and thus to have our share in the work of truth.

⁹I did write to the church; but Diotrephes, who enjoys being their leader, ignores us. ¹⁰Therefore, if I come I will speak publicly of what he is doing in spreading evil nonsense about us. And that is not all. Not only does he refuse to welcome the brothers himself but he even hinders those who wish to do so and expels them from the church!

¹¹Beloved, do not imitate what is evil but what is good. Whoever does what is good belongs to God; whoever does what is evil has never seen God. ¹²Demetrius is one who gets a good testimonial from all, even from truth itself. We give our testimonial as well, and you know that our testimony is true.

¹³There is much more that I had in mind to write you, but I do not wish to write it out with pen and ink. ¹⁴Rather, I hope to see you soon, when we can talk face to face.

¹⁵Peace be with you. The beloved here send you their greetings; greet the beloved there, each by name.

(*Again, before studying what follows, please read and reread, slowly and aloud, the Third Epistle of John itself.*)

Structure: The Third Epistle of John is another brief note, slightly shorter than 2 John, and with similar divisions: the introduction (v. 1); the note of happiness (vv. 2-4); the body (vv. 5-12), which centers successively on Gaius, Diotrephes, and Demetrius; the conclusion (vv. 13-15).

Occasion and contents: This letter is addressed to an individual, Gaius, a member of another Johannine church, of whom visitors to the author have spoken well (vv. 3, 6). The purpose of the letter is to congratulate Gaius (vv. 2-4) while encouraging his continued support for Johannine missionaries (vv. 5-8), such as Demetrius, who probably has been sent by the author himself (v. 12) and is the bearer of this letter. The author also wishes

124

o warn Gaius against Diotrephes, who has taken leadership in one of the ohannine groups and refuses to afford hospitality to the missionaries. Even worse, he expels from the church those Christians who do help them.

The epistle, consequently, centers on hospitality and authority, not on the Christological and soteriological problems evident in 1 and 2 John. Yet the same author seems to have written all three, and at approximately the same time. We have already seen how 2 John is linked to 1 John. 3 John, on its part, is linked to 2 John both by the designation of the author as "the elder" and by the close similarity of 3 John 13-14 to 2 John 12. There is a further fascinating similarity between 3 John 12b: ". . . and you know that our testimony is true," and the Gospel of John 21:24: ". . . and we know that his testimony is true," which provides argument for those who believe that the Johannine epistles were written by the redactor of the Fourth Gospel, whose hand is seen most clearly in John 21.

Comments: (a) About Gaius (v. 1) absolutely nothing is known except what is told us in this letter. That he is one of the author's "children" (v. 4) has suggested to some commentators that he owed his conversion to the author, but "children" is used so often in these epistles that it need not carry such specific meaning.

b) Verses 5-8 give us a picture of early Christian missionaries, whose subsistence depends completely on the hospitality provided by fellow Christians. Those who do afford such aid should be considered co-workers (v. 8).

c) Most of the scholarly conjecture regarding 3 John concerns Diotrephes. Of him nothing is known except the few particulars given in verses 9-10. His precise position vis-à-vis the elder is uncertain, though there is no lack of suggestions on the part of scholars.

i) Some believe that he had assumed a position of authoritative leadership, much like that of a bishop, and was firmly opposed to the itinerant missionaries deriving their authority from "the elder."

ii) Others suggest that the difficulty concerned doctrine, and that Diotrephes was an innovator and a heretical teacher. In that case, however, it is surprising that the author makes no specific mention of false teaching.

iii) Still others believe that the shoe should be put on the other foot and that the author himself was the innovator.

All that is known for certain, however, is contained in our text: Diotrephes did not acknowledge the elder's authority, claiming precedence for himself; he refused to welcome the missionaries and expelled those who did; he appears to be opposed by Gaius and the others (vv. 5-8, 10, 15) who have welcomed the missionaries. These particulars lead us to support the opinion (i) that Diotrephes had become overly authoritative, challenging the position of even "the elder."

d) Demetrius is evidently one of the Johannine missionaries sent out by the author and probably carrying along this letter.

e) Verses 13-14 are almost identical to 2 John 12, an indication of the same authorship.

f) Verse 15 gives us a view of one Johannine community saluting another. On both sides, the church members are the beloved, the friends, *hoi philoi*. The author has written to keep these friends united and their church intact.

REVIEW AIDS AND DISCUSSION TOPICS

I

1:1-4:45 Introduction; New Beginnings (*pages* 6-22)

1. What does the Gospel of John tell us about God's self-revelation in 1:1-18? What is the purpose of all the testimonies in 1:19-51?
2. What is the overall theological emphasis of Episode I (2:1-4:42)?
3. What is the theology of the Cana story (2:1-12)? In what sense does Jesus manifest his "glory" (2:11)? Why does John speak of "signs"?
4. What is the theology of the temple narrative (2:13-25)? What time indication is found here? What do the other Gospels say about this incident?
5. What is the theology of the Nicodemus incident (3:1-36)? What is strange about the dialogue? Is Nicodemus a true believer? To what does "be lifted up" in 3:14 refer?
6. What is the theology of the story about the Samaritan woman (4:1-42)? How were the Samaritans related to the Jews? In what ways are the humanness of both Jesus and the woman expressed? Why did the Samaritan townsfolk believe?

II

4:46-6:71 Jesus' Life-giving Word; Jesus as the Bread of Life (*pages* 23-35)

1. How is all the material of 4:46-5:47 linked together? What is its theological emphasis? In what ways is this important for us today?
2. What two questions does the evangelist treat in 4:46-5:47 (see 5:18)? What divine actions does Jesus perform? Does this mean that there are two Gods? How does the evangelist face up to this problem?
3. Why does the miracle of the loaves appear in all four Gospels? What is its theological bi-level here?
4. Which verse gives the text for the homily on life-giving bread in 6:26-59? How is the homily developed? What do the important words "believe . . . eat . . . drink" indicate?
5. What two models does the evangelist offer us in 6:66-71? Does he insist on hierarchy?

III

7:1–10:42 Identity Crisis; Light of the World; Sight and Blindness (*pages* 35–53)

1. What are the two questions of chapter 7? Of chapter 8? What historical bi-levels are evident in these two chapters?
2. In which Old Testament book is the profound meaning of I AM best illustrated? Discuss that meaning.
3. How could the story of the blind man (9:1-41) help catechumens today? By what stages does the blind man progress in faith? What does this statement mean: "We find in chapter 9 the most outstanding example in John of the use of historical bi-levels"?
4. Why does the account of the good shepherd follow the story of the man born blind? Is it out of place? Which Old Testament book does it reflect?
5. What is "Hanukkah"? What question about Jesus is being asked in 10:24-38?

IV

11:1–12:50 Life over Death; Life Through Death (*pages* 53–63)

1. What is the central theological teaching of the story of Martha and Mary (11:1-44)? What is the great profession of faith in this story?
2. What other theological motifs are evident in this account?
3. In what way does the story of Lazarus in chapter 11 prepare the reader for chapter 20?
4. What new followers of Jesus are introduced in 12:20-36? How does this fit with the theologies of "the grain of wheat" in v. 24 and the being "lifted up" in v. 32?
5. What themes of the first twelve chapters are summarized in 12:44-50?

V

13:1–17:26 The Farewell Discourses (*pages* 63–80)

1. Why is the second half of this Gospel called "The Book of Glory"? How does it differ from the first half, "The Book of Signs"?
2. Discuss what "the world" means in the Fourth Gospel.
3. What does the word "Paraclete" mean? What will be the function of the Paraclete? What role does the Paraclete play in your life today?
4. Jesus' prayer in chapter 17 is often called his "Priestly Prayer." Is this a good title? Why? Can you find one all-important petition in this prayer?
5. Why is there no Eucharist at John's Last Supper?

VI

18:1–20:31 The Passion Narrative and the Resurrection (*pages* 81–97)

1. What are some of the differences between John's account of Jesus' passion and death and those of the other three Gospels?
2. Discuss the possible significance of the incident described in 19:25-27.
3. What are the Johannine peculiarities in the description of Jesus' death (19:28-37)? What is remarkable about the burial?
4. How does John structure the resurrection account (ch. 20)? Do the various characters believe? In recording their reactions, what is John saying to his fellow Christians and to us?

VII

21:1-25 The Resurrection Appearance in Galilee; Conclusions (pages 97-104)

1. What is unusual about this chapter? Who are the participants? Why "153" fish?
2. What portrayal is made of Peter? Why the triple profession in verses 15-17? Why the charcoal fire (v. 9)?
3. How are the evangelist's teachings about God's self-revelation, about mission, and about the Paraclete all related?
4. Who was the Beloved Disciple?
5. Give a thumbnail sketch of John's community.

VIII

1 John 1:1-3:24 Prologue; Sin; The Commandments; False Teachers (pages 105-114)

1. Upon what does the Prologue (1:1-4) insist?
2. What does the author teach about sin in 1:5-2:2? How does the epistle differ in this section from the Fourth Gospel?
3. Is the commandment of love old or new (2:3-17)? Who are the "little ones"? the "young men"? the "fathers"? What is the "world" of which this epistle speaks?
4. Who are the antichrists (2:18-27)? What major crisis has occasioned the author's concern? In general, what was the issue of contention?
5. What does this epistle ask us to do (2:18-3:24)? In what sense is 3:23 the heart of this epistle?

IX

1 John 4:1-5:21 The Two Spirits; God's Love; Faith; Summary; Conclusions (pages 114-121)

1. What is our author's test for orthodox teaching (4:1-6)? Is his opposition having any success?
2. What description of God is given in 4:7-21? What challenge is offered to us? What creedal elements appear in this epistle?
3. What are the testimonies to Jesus in 5:1-13? Are they historical or sacramental?
4. What is 1 John's teaching about prayer (5:14-21)?
5. Why was this epistle written? Who wrote it? When?
6. What is the central theological issue of 1 John? Discuss its moral teaching.
7. What is the function of the Paraclete in 1 John as compared with the Fourth Gospel?

X

2 John 1-13; 3 John 1-15 The Second and Third Epistles of John (pages 122-125)

1. How is 2 John related to 1 John? Why was 2 John written?
2. What are the author's two insistent recommendations in 2 John?
3. What are the two central issues of 3 John?
4. What might the similarity between 3 John 12b and John 21:24 indicate?
5. Why was the Third Epistle of John written?